Ripples In The Lake

Of Eternity

GW00727974

Pointers To Realizing

and Loving

The Source of Being

Based on the Meditations, Investigations, Contemplations
and Experiences
of over Forty Years of Spiritual Search and Practice
By Colin Drake

Published by Beyond Awakening Publications, Tomewin

Cover design, photography and other titles by the author:

Beyond the Separate Self
The End of Anxiety and Mental Suffering

A Light Unto The Self
Self Discovery Through Investigation of Experience

Awakening and Beyond
Self-Recognition and its Consequences

Awareness of Awareness - The Open Way

The Happiness That Needs Nothing
Pointers to That Which is Always Here

Freedom From Anxiety and Needless Suffering

The Simplicity of Awakening

Poetry From Beyond The Separate Self

Poetry From Being A Light Unto The Self

Poetry From Awakening and Beyond

Poetry From Awareness of Awareness

Poetry From The Happiness That Needs Nothing

Humanity Our Place in the Universe
The Central Beliefs of the Worlds Religions

All of these titles are available as: e-books and in hard copy at
http://www.lulu.com/spotlight/ColinDrake

Contents

Introduction

What follows is vital to 'new readers' whereas, those of my previous books may skip to the 'Overview' if they wish. This is not advisable unless they have realized that, at the deepest level, they are Pure Awareness – the constant conscious subjective presence. Also the first portion contains information regarding the framework within which this book was written and its objectives, which I hope would be of interest to all readers.

Introduction

The main aim of this book is to act as a stand-alone guide to, and practices for, Awakening. It is composed of articles, resulting from my further investigations (and contemplations) into the nature of Reality and replies to questions since the publication of *The Simplicity of Awakening*. The thrust of the book is that beneath the surface appearance of thoughts (including all mental activity) and sensations there is a deeper level of being, which is the perceiver of these. The former are a flow of fleeting objects whereas the latter, which is the Awareness of these, is a constant conscious subjective presence. This is the only constant that has been (with) you since you were born and that which has witnessed your entire life. Therefore it would be more accurate to say that this is **what you actually are** rather than the ever changing body/mind in which these thoughts and sensations have occurred. In fact the thoughts and sensations are the direct experience of this body/mind and the Awareness is how you 'know' them.

This Awareness can be likened to a backlit 'screen' displaying the thoughts and sensations, occurring a any given moment, that the mind views and then decides which of these it will focus on and 'process'. Or, for the purpose of this book, like a lake (of Consciousness) in which the ripples are the thoughts and sensations which are occurring in Consciousness itself. Actually This is nondual ('not two' or more …) and thus all Awareness of thoughts and sensations is a facet of the lake of Consciousness itself, and thus not personal, although at the level of body/mind it may appear to be so. When one sees that this Awareness is the deepest level of our being and identifies with, and as, this rather than with the ever changing flow of thoughts and sensations then this constitutes an awakening. For one realizes that the apparent separate self of body/mind and self-image is an illusion occurring in the common, constant, conscious, presence … that is the 'lake' of Awareness – Consciousness at rest, in which ripples (movements) arise, abide and subside. These movements constitute the cosmic energy of which all manifestation is an 'expression'. For modern physics has shown that matter **is** energy, which is synonymous with, and entails, motion.

Then this realization needs to be established by repeated Awakenings due to the natural tendency to 'nod off' and re-identify oneself as a separate object in a universe of separate objects. When one is awake then anxiety and unnecessary mental suffering disappear, for these are caused by this misidentification which causes us to see each other, and the world, through a murky filter of self-interest, self-concern, self-promotion, self-aggrandizement, self-loathing, the list is almost endless. It is this world-view that causes the anxiety and mental suffering based on concern for the future and feeling we are bound by the past.

On Awakening one discovers that there truly is no separate self and so this filter is removed allowing us to see the world 'as it is' with no self-concern for the future or past. When one fully realises that there is no separate individual self then all the needless burdens of self-image, self-importance, self-promotion, self-interest, self-cherishing, self-hate, self-loathing, self-anything ... are lifted and remain so as long as one remains awake in this realisation. This gives a great ease and lightness of being which is (en) lightenment in the literal sense of the word...

The main thrust of this (and all of my) book(s) is that of self-identity – who, or what, are we in essence? What is it that is at the core of our being, deeper than the surface level of mind/body, thoughts and sensations? To discover this is vital, for without a clear idea of one's essential identity one cannot relate to the world, and others, in an appropriate way. For, if we believe that we are separate objects, in a universe of separate objects, then we will naturally treat ourselves and others as objects, which I think we can see to be an unsatisfactory arrangement. For this tends to lead to blatant self-interest and exploitation of our fellow beings, the outcome of which is apparent in the modern world.

So the quest is to inquire and discover that which is beyond objectification, the deeper level that is the perceiver, the subjective level in which objects (thoughts and sensations) come and go.

The easiest way to find out is to investigate our moment to moment experience, which reveals that our deepest essence is Awareness, and the framework for this investigation is given in appendix one. At this stage we need to become clear as to the meaning of the term 'awareness' which has two meanings which we must not confuse. The phrase 'awareness of Awareness' utilises both of these meanings and for this reason I have used a capital letter (when using this expression) for the second one so that they may be easily distinguished in what follows[1].

The first occurrence (awareness) is synonymous with mindfulness, that is 'seeing' with the mind, or keeping (something) in the mind. It also means 'becoming conscious of', noticing, or perceiving, as in 'I became aware of …' This is the normal everyday usage as in the OED definition of 'aware' – *having knowledge or perception of …*

So the term 'awareness of Awareness' means becoming conscious, or having knowledge or perception, of Awareness. We now need to define this Awareness which is simply the total 'seeing' and perceiving (or seer and perceiver) of everything detected by the mind and senses, whereas awareness (becoming aware of) is the partial 'seeing' of those thoughts/sensations on which the mind is focussed, or which are noticed. So these are not different, awareness just being a limited version (or incidence) of Awareness.

This is easy to directly experience by closing one's eyes and seeing whether you can simultaneously be 'aware of' (notice) all of the

---

[1] In general, throughout all of my books, whenever I use the word 'awareness' I am using this as Awareness (The Totality which is 'aware' of all) unless it is in the phrase 'awareness of Awareness' which the following discussion addresses.

thoughts/mental images and sensations that are occurring. This is found to be impossible and yet these are all there in Awareness, which becomes apparent when one focuses one's mind on , or turns one's mind to, any of them.... and there they are! I expanded on this in 'The Problem' chapter one of *Beyond The Separate Self* and, for the sake of completeness, have included it in this book as a prologue.

This Awareness is the constant conscious subjective presence in which our thoughts/mental images and sensations arise, abide, are spied and subside. Before every one of them Awareness is present, during each one of them they are 'seen' by This and This is still here after they go. Just check this out now – notice that before each thought/sensation there is Awareness of 'what is' (the totality of these at any given moment) , during each of these there is Awareness of them within 'what is' and after each of them has gone there is still Awareness of 'what is'.

Rumi described this as: *the clear conscious core of your being, the same in ecstasy as in self-hating fatigue.* That is to say the Awareness in which the ecstasy or the self-hating fatigue appears. Now generally you would just be aware of, and affected by, the phenomenal state. If, however, you become aware of the Awareness in which this state is occurring and can fully identify with, and as, this Awareness then the state loses its power to affect your equanimity. For Awareness is always utterly still and silent, totally unaffected by whatever appears in it, in the same way that the sky is unaffected by the clouds that scud across it or a lake is unchanged by the ripples that move across its surface.

It is this identification with Awareness that can be achieved by 'investigation of our moment to moment experience', see the appendix. When this is successfully accomplished and you can see that at the deepest level, <u>you are Awareness itself</u> then this is an Awakening. If this cultivated by remaining 'aware of Awareness' (and identified as Awareness) then this leads to full Awakening.

At this stage it would be advisable to carry this out by following the instructions provided in the appendix. When this is successfully undertaken one becomes aware of the constant, conscious, subjective presence – Pure Awareness – that is at the centre of our being. Following from this is the realization that, as That, we are instruments through which That can sense, contemplate, experience, engage with, act in, and enjoy the physical world. This realization is dealt within the second appendix and it would be advisable to consider that now.

These appendices come from previous works but are necessary inclusions so that the reader may approach this book with the requisite preparation, and also to make this work complete in itself.

Each chapter should be treated as an aid to your enquiry into the nature of Reality, and as such should not just be read and intellectually considered but need to be taken slowly, step by step, not moving onto the next step until one fully 'sees' the step that is being considered. This does not mean to say that one needs to agree with each statement, as any investigation is personal, but one needs to understand what is being said. Also to get the most out of each chapter one needs to spend some time contemplating it until one 'feels' what it is pointing to; if a chapter is just read without due attention then its significance may well be missed.

If the results of your investigations are that you discover the Pure Awareness that is at the core of your being and can identify with, and as, This then this is an Awakening. However, this Awakening will be readily veiled by one's previous identification with the body/mind. To overcome this one needs to:

> be committed to completely identifying with the deeper level of Pure Awareness, for in this there is always perfect peace and repose. Before this complete identification with Pure Awareness is established one will flip/flop between identifying with Awareness and identifying with a mind/body. Awakening is an ongoing process with complete identification with Pure Awareness as the final goal. For it is in fact a series of Awakenings, which is very necessary due to our natural tendency to go back to sleep! Every time we 'flop' back to identifying ourselves as mind/body we have nodded off again;

and so the 'flip' to identifying with the deeper level of our being is another Awakening. The author knows this only too well, and makes no claim to 'lack of sleep'. As one investigates and cultivates this deeper level, the periods of 'wakefulness' are prolonged and consequently one 'nods off' less. The period of time between one's first Awakening and being completely awake is indeterminate and varies greatly from being to being. However, this is not a problem, for as the periods of 'wakefulness' (which are totally carefree) increase so will the commitment to identifying with the level of Pure Awareness. This will lead to more reflection and investigation, resulting in further Awakenings which will continue the process. To call it a process may seem a misnomer for when one is 'awake' there's no process going on, but the continual naps keep the whole thing running.

This commitment to identifying with the level of Pure Awareness involves having faith in our body/mind to negotiate living in the world, for this is what it has evolved to do. This 'complete identification' will not happen all at once but is something that has to be cultivated. I would recommend doing this by spending three periods of at least twenty minutes, every day, totally relaxing into the recognition of Pure Awareness. For an example of a format for this see chapter one. The best times for this are between getting up and engaging in one's daily

activities, after the day's work is over and just before going to
sleep. The first 'sets one up' for the day, the second refreshes
and re-energises one after the day's toil, and the third aids in
achieving a deep and peaceful night's sleep. One may argue
that there is not enough time available for this, but these
meditations provide so much relaxation and recharging that one
can easily recover the time by sleeping for an hour less.[2]

So Awakening is not for the dilettante, the dabbler, but is a full-time
proposition.

A later theme of the book is to develop love of the Absolute, the source,
by nurturing love of the manifestation by the Absolute and vice-versa.
For we are expressions of the Absolute in a manifest body/mind and
thus have the potential to achieve, or realize, this. In these discussions
the Absolute, Consciousness at rest, is called 'the lover' and the
manifestation 'the beloved'. There is a discussion regarding the 'ways'
of knowledge and love, followed by three simple practices to enable us
to feel and develop this love in both directions, that of the lover for the
beloved and vice-versa.

One other thing that should be noted is that this book is mostly
composed of individual articles and replies to questions. They are
given as pointers and aids for the reader's own investigations into, and

---

[2] C.Drake, *Beyond The Separate Self*, 2009, Tomewin, p.89-90

contemplations on, the problem of self-identity. There is necessarily some duplication between them as what is being discussed is so simple. They are different 'takes' on the same simplicity, presenting the material in various ways whilst building upon what has been discovered, so some repetition is unavoidable. It should also be noted that each of these are, as far as is possible, stand-alone meditations or contemplations, thus needing to make sense by themselves. Therefore some sections of each will contain similar passages, so that they are relatively complete when read in isolation.

If you have any questions, comments, or feedback you are welcome to contact me at colinj108@gmail.com .

Overview

As usual this book is composed of articles and replies to questions written since the publication of my last - *The Simplicity of Awakening.* The title is from an article which sprang from the realization that one only becomes 'aware of Awareness' by the 'things' appearing in it. So I know that Awareness is present because I am aware of my thoughts and sensations. This led me to compare Awareness to an infinite lake, reflecting the sky, which is only apparent when ripples appear in it, at other times it is indistinguishable from the sky – see cover photo. There are also chapters considering many different traditions from the nondual point of view such as the Native American, the Trinity in Christianity, the uses of 'Om Namah Shivaya' in Hinduism and some on Buddhism.

At the suggestion of my reviewer, Ramaji, I also included a section on love which gives an overview of the two approaches 'Love and Knowledge' and a chapter which posits that 'Love is All there Is'; followed by three practices for developing (and experiencing) love for the Source (Consciousness) and for experiencing how this Source uses our body/minds in love for (with) its own manifestation.

Finally, there are three different approaches to the (thrice) daily 'practice' I recommend of totally relaxing into 'awareness of

Awareness'. These are from three different initial mind-states: firstly when the mind is already relaxed and one-pointed, secondly from when it is in its usual busy state and finally from when it is deluged by a torrent of thought. So now the book has a symmetry, giving three ways of 'loving the beloved' and also three ways of 'relaxing into awareness of Awareness', thus giving bhakti (love) and jnana (knowledge) even 'weight'.

Chapter Synopsis

The preface describes the problem with identifying as a separate object, how this occurs and points to how this may be overcome. This is reprinted from *Beyond The Separate Self* and may be skipped by readers of that book.

The prologue likens Consciousness to an infinite lake in which the ripples are 'things', as manifestation is cosmic energy - that is motion in Consciousness, which appear in Awareness, Consciousness at rest. So just as ripples arise in, abide in and subside back into the lake so manifestation arises in, abides in and subsides back into Consciousness.

Chapter one gives two simple methods (among many) for relaxing into 'awareness of Awareness' - a practice which I advise those who have had an awakening, by becoming aware of (and identified with) Awareness, to undertake thrice daily. For a more 'freestyle method' when the mind is seemingly full of thoughts see chapter twenty four - A *Morning Contemplation/Relaxation.*

Chapter two is a discussion on the subject of the mechanism of our moment to moment experience and the response that this engenders.

Chapter three gives a modern fix for misidentification based on the 'switching of users' when logged on to a computer.

Chapter four discusses the need to be loyal, or true, to Awakening in order to remain 'awake'.

Chapter five is a discussion about judging 'others' and how this requires for the 'judge' to be misidentified for this to occur.

Chapter six insists that 'awakening' is available to all and not restricted to a 'chosen' few.

Chapter seven discusses why most people are not interested in 'awakening'.

Chapter eight considers the paradox that 'awakening' occurs by identifying with Pure Awareness, which is omnipresent and omniscient, but that this does not lead to personal omnipresence and omniscience.

Chapter nine gives a method for dealing with self hatred and discusses how this is a prime indicator of misidentification.

Chapter ten considers the Christian Trinity giving a non-dual interpretation of this.

Chapter eleven is a modified letter written by a Japanese twelfth century Buddhist monk which discusses attaining Buddhahood in this lifetime.

Chapter telve elucidates the 'radiance of Awareness', explaining how this manifests and can be 'seen'.

Chapter thirteen is a commentary on two well known folk/spiritual songs which share a common tune.

Chapter fourteen discusses nonduality and Native American Spirituality based on the writings of Ohiyesa of the native Dakota, Sioux Nation.

Chapter fifteen gives multiple uses for the mantra 'Om Namah Sivaya' – Hail Pure Awareness, The Totality of Being.

Chapter sixteen talks about the 'tricky mind' and gives three examples of how it tries to remain in control by trivializing, or overlooking, 'awakening'.

Chapter seventeen gives the antidote to the 'tricky mind' by honoring what has been discovered and seeing all of its tricks as ephemeral thoughts appearing in Awareness.

Chapter eighteen is an email discussion about (Vipassana) meditation resulting from a response to my article 'The Tricky Mind'.

Chapter nineteen gives an introduction to Vipassana meditation, which is widely practiced, by considering a book on the subject by Joseph Goldstein – a famous Vipassana teacher. This teacher is referenced in the previous chapter as being one with a more 'open' approach to Vipassana.

Chapter twenty proposes that Vipassana meditation does not go far enough as it does not address the question of self-identity - 'who am I'? Further Tibetan and Zen breath awareness meditation, which does address this, fails to consider the function of human beings as expressions, and instruments of, The Absolute.

Chapter twenty one discusses how the 'paths' of knowledge , Jnana Yoga, and love, Bhakti Yoga, lead to the same result.

Chapter twenty two posits that 'love is no separation' and in the Absolute (Consciousness at rest and in motion, which is all there is) there is no separation and thus love.

The next three chapters are devoted to love of the Absolute, the source, by Its manifestation (you!) and to love of Its manifestation by the Absolute. In this discussion the Absolute, Consciousness at rest, is called 'the lover' and the manifestation 'the beloved'. The first of these, chapter twenty three, deals with concentrating on, and enjoying/loving, one sensation – that of feelings in, and on the surface of, the body.

Chapter twenty four expands on the previous one by becoming aware of, and enjoying, all of the five senses one at a time. This leads to the lover loving the beloved, which is then reversed by using the mind (a facet of the beloved) to investigate Awareness (the lover) Itself. The result of this is that the beloved gets to 'know' and love the lover. So that the whole practice is one by which the lover and beloved can 'know' and love each other. Or to put it another way by which Consciousness can 'know' and love Itself in both 'modes' when at rest (as Pure Awareness) and when in motion (as Its manifestation).

In chapter twenty five the previous practice is expanded into one in which the senses are enjoyed, or loved by the lover, one at a time and then 'laid over' the preceding one(s), so that at the end the lover is enjoying all five senses together.

Chapter twenty six is one in which In which I answer the question 'do you give Satsang?' and enclose other information regarding accessing more articles, poems, book info and reviews, my interview on youtube and joining my email group.

Chapter twenty seven was added just to get the book back on track, an example of a morning's contemplation/relaxation into 'awareness of Awareness'.

Preface– The Problem

A general discussion on the problem of identifying oneself as an individual object in a universe of multiple objects. It also sets the framework for the investigations that follow which reveal a deeper level of being than that of thoughts and sensations.

The Problem

For most of us much of our waking time is spent in obsessive thinking about 'ourselves' and our relationships with other people. This is especially true when we are not working, using our minds in a productive activity; or when we are not relaxing in such a way that engages the mind such as reading a book, playing a game or watching a screen. For the mind is akin to an onboard-computer which is a wonderful tool for problem-solving, information storing, retrieval and processing, and evaluating the data provided by our senses. However, when it is not fully utilized it tends to search for other problems to solve, and if these are not presently available it tends to speculate about the future, delve into the past, or imagine in the present, creating non-existent problems which it then tries to solve!

Most people tend to identify with their mind, rather than seeing it as a tool, which creates myriad problems. This causes everything to be seen through the filter of the mind: its opinions, judgements, and self-interest. When this happens we cease to see things as they really are which lessens our ability to relate to the world in a natural healthy way. Imagine the problems it would cause if your computer decided that it was 'you' and coloured all the information it retrieved from the internet with its own arbitrary opinions and judgements. In this case you would be unable to rely on any of this information, and if you did then any decisions made using this would be liable to be faulty.

In the above example 'you' are obviously not the computer but the perceiver of the data provided by the computer and all of its multimedia functionality. In the same way, we have a deeper level of being than the mind (thoughts and mental images) and body (physical sensations), which is also the perceiver of this 'data'. However, when we identify at the surface level of mind/body we are unaware of this and tend to suffer due to the shortcomings of our mind/body. This is akin to suffering because our computer is not the most up-to-date, fastest attractive model available.

This is exactly what most of us do, worrying about our body-image and mental capacity and ability. We tend to expand our concept of self-identity to include an imaginary self-image consisting of our physical appearance, mental ability, status, occupation, position in society, family situation, achievements, lack of achievements, ambitions, hopes, fears, memories and projections into the future. Not only do we consider this to be who or what we are, and continually obsess about this, but we also spend large periods of time comparing this with the equally erroneous images we have formed of other people we relate to.

So we have identified ourselves as an imaginary object, in a universe of separate objects, which we then compare with other imaginary objects! This is bound to lead to confusion, suffering and an increased feeling of separation, which is exacerbated by the fact that we do not even see these other objects as they actually are, but as we imagine them to be through the filter of our mind's opinions, judgements and self-interest.

To free ourselves from this nightmarish scenario and the continual obsession with the 'separate self' we imagine ourselves to be, we need to connect with the deeper level of our being as the 'subject' rather than an 'object', where we are the perceiver of our thoughts and sensations. This level is ever-present as there is continual awareness of our thoughts and sensations. Whilst we identify with the mind this level is overlooked; the mind continues the vicious circle of obsessive thinking by processing these thoughts and sensations and relating them to the imaginary self-image that it has concocted.

However, we can easily escape from this vicious circle by simply investigating the nature and relationship of these thoughts and sensations and our awareness of them. When this is fully accomplished we discover that, at the deepest level, we are the perceiver of these thoughts and sensations. These are just ephemeral objects which come and go, leaving the perceiver totally unaffected, in the same way that the sky is unaffected by the clouds which scud across it, or the ocean is undisturbed by the waves and swells that appear on its surface. The framework for this investigation is given in appendix one and, if you have not carried this out yet, it is advisable to do this practice now before continuing.

This book is designed to provide pointers which will help to take one beyond the 'separate self' we have imagined ourselves to be. In this we discover that most of our worries have no foundation for they are just the mind projecting into the future, wallowing in the past, or obsessing over the imaginary self-image it has conjured up. Once the mind is put in its place - as the servant and not the master - we start to see things as they truly are, and to recognize not only the deeper level of being within ourselves but also to recognize this in those around us. Then we see that our self-image and the images we have created of other people are all just illusions. At this deeper level we relate to others in a much more loving, wholesome way, for it becomes clear that there is in fact no separation between ourselves and others, as at this level we share the same constant conscious subjective presence.

This is not a question of belief or imagination but of discovery by direct investigation, and for this to be effective we need to put aside all belief systems and acquired knowledge concerning who we are at the underlying level beyond thoughts and sensations. The only knowledge of this that is valid is that which is revealed to each one of us by direct experience. The easiest way for this direct experience to occur is by enquiring into the nature of experience itself, and for this enquiry to be effective we need to start from the position of believing and knowing nothing.

The chapters that follow are aids to this enquiry, and as such should not just be read and intellectually considered but need to be taken slowly, step by step, not moving onto the next step until one fully 'sees' the step that is being considered. This does not mean to say that one needs to agree with each statement, as any investigation is personal, but one needs to understand what is being said. Also to get the most out of each chapter one needs to spend some time contemplating it until one 'feels' what it is pointing to; if a chapter is just read without due attention then its significance may well be missed.

The Problem

Before starting we need to discuss the nature of awareness itself. It is obvious that we would not 'know' (be aware of) our own perceptions without awareness being present. This does not mean that we are always conscious of each one of them, as this is dictated by where we put our attention, or upon what we focus our mind. However, all sensations detected by the body are there in awareness, and we can readily become conscious of them by turning our attention to them. It is also true that our thoughts and mental images immediately appear in awareness, but these require less attention to be seen as they occur in the mind itself. So awareness is like the screen on which all of our thoughts and sensations appear, and the mind becomes conscious of these by focusing on them. Take, for example, what happens when you open your eyes and look at a beautiful view: everything seen immediately appears in awareness, but for the mind to make anything of this it needs to focus upon certain elements of what is seen. 'There is an amazing tree', 'wow look at that eagle', 'what a stunning sky', etc. To be sure, you may just make a statement like 'what a beautiful view', but this does not in itself say much and is so self-evident as to be not worth saying!

The point is that the mind is a tool for problem-solving, information storing, retrieval and processing, and evaluating the data provided by our senses. It achieves this by focusing on specific sensations, thoughts or mental images that are present in awareness, and 'processing' these. In fact we only truly see 'things as they are' when they are not seen through the filter of the mind, and this occurs when what is encountered is able to 'stop the mind'. For instance we have all had glimpses of this at various times in our lives, often when seeing a beautiful sunset, a waterfall or some other wonderful natural phenomenon. These may seem other-worldly or intensely vivid, until the mind kicks in with any evaluation when everything seems to return to 'normal'. In fact nature is much more vivid and alive when directly perceived, and the more we identify with the 'perceiver', as awareness itself, the more frequently we see things 'as they are'.

However, as long as we identify with our imaginary self-image we are always trying to better ourselves, achieve more - knowledge, possessions, power, fame, etc. - polish this self-image and generally build ourselves up. This tends to make us live in the future and stops us living fully in the present moment. The other side of this coin is to live in regret as to what might have been, self-loathing, melancholy or nostalgia and yearning for the past. This, once again, stops us seeing 'what is' here and now, either by making us live in the past or by the mind spinning on our failures and lack of self-worth.

The following chapters are aids in the investigation of one's moment-to-moment experience. These are designed to enable you to discover this deeper level of being where you are truly the 'perceiver' not the 'perceived'.

Prologue – Ripples In The Lake

Images Consciousness as an infinite lake in which the ripples are 'things', as manifestation is cosmic energy - that is motion in Consciousness, which appear in Awareness, Consciousness at rest. So just as ripples arise in, abide in and subside back into the lake so manifestation arises in, abides in and subsides back into Consciousness.

Imagine a limitless lake, serene and unruffled, stretching to the horizon and immaculately reflecting a completely clear, and cloudless, azure blue sky. In this scenario the lake would be invisible as it would totally merge with its surroundings and no separation would be apparent. Now see what happens when ripples occur, for whatever reason, immediately the lake appears visible as its reflections become distorted and wavy.

Pure Awareness, Consciousness at rest, is like this lake aware of and reflecting everything, the ripples, that appear in it. In our direct experience the 'things' that appear in it are sensations and thoughts (including mental images). The mind is always looking at this 'lake of Awareness' noticing those things that it thinks are important and need to be processed. It is interesting to note that, as pointed out, the 'lake' cannot be seen without the ripples but the mind still does not see it as it is more concerned with processing the 'ripples'.

When one is identified with, and as, the mind/body - that is as a separate 'self' - then the lake is always disturbed by background 'swell' of the opinionated self and self-interest, self-concern, self-aggrandizement, self-promotion, self-loathing … the list is endless. This means that the 'ripples' are not seen 'as they are', for this 'swell' distorts them even more and thus the processing of them can well lead to erroneous conclusions.

However, when one becomes aware of the existence of this 'lake of Awareness' and can truly see that this is the constant conscious subjective presence in which our sensations/thoughts come and go, ebb and flow, to and fro, then there is the possibility for correct identification to occur. For it can be easily seen that this 'aware presence' is all that has been with us since we were born and has witnessed the pantomime of our entire lives. All of our experiences, memories, thoughts and sensations are (and have been) a flow of ephemeral objects appearing in this presence … that is ripples in the 'lake of Awareness'. Thus one can see that, at the deepest level, one **is** this 'aware presence' and never separate from this 'lake' whilst the flow of objects are just ripples rising in, abiding in and subsiding back into this.

When this identification occurs, and one can truly see that the 'separate self' is an illusion, then the distorting 'swell' caused by misidentification subsides and things can be seen 'as they are' with no grasping, clinging, fear or avoidance – as they are seen to be just fleeting occurrences with no intrinsic meaning. This in turn enables for them to be processed spontaneously by the mind without referring to a background store of small self and its opinions, thus making the resulting conclusions and response more natural and error free. This means that we do not 'wobble' when making decisions and are not beset by the curse of 'second thought' caused by the previously mentioned 'swell' which can cause much indecision and prevarication. It also means that we do not have to reference everything by a set of rules, or precepts, for the true Self – Pure Awareness, can be trusted to respond to every situation in an appropriate way. Then your 'song-bird can fly freely' (Khalil Gibran) for your conduct will not be defined by ethics but by the spontaneity of The Self.[3]

When 'wobbling', second thought or unnecessary suffering reoccur this means that we have once again identified with the 'ripples', that is sensation/thoughts – mind/body. The solution to this is to reinvestigate one's own direct experience (now!), see the appendix, which reveals the constant conscious subject presence, (the lake of) Pure Awareness that we truly **are**. I also recommend relaxing into the realization of 'awareness of Awareness' for at least 20 minutes three times a day until awakening is fully established and misidentification no longer occurs. It is interesting to note that to become 'aware of (the lake of) Awareness' requires noting that one is aware (there is awareness) of the 'ripples' which proves that Awareness is already present.

For, as previously discussed, the lake is 'invisible' (even from the mind) when there are no ripples present. An easy technique for practicing 'awareness of Awareness' is given in 'Three Phases of Liberation' (in *Freedom From Anxiety and Needless Suffering*) which entails: seeing 'what is', which reveals (the lake of) Awareness, resulting in the relaxation which is the outcome of realising that there is nothing to achieve, find or get as Awareness is always already present and **is** the essential level of our being. The first step of this, seeing 'what is', requires noting that one is aware of the' ripples', as discussed

---

[3] See 'Awakening and Ethics' in 'Awareness of Awareness – The Open Way'.

above. Therefore the 'ripples' are vital in revealing the presence of the 'lake' in which they are occurring and in fact everything in manifestation may be used in this way, for more on this see 'Every perception reveals reality' in *Beyond the Separate Self.*

Awareness can also be described as Consciousness at rest in which all manifestation (cosmic energy – movements in This) arises, abides, is spied and subsides. For all motion arises in (and from) stillness, exists in, and can be seen relative to this, and returns back into this when its energy is expended. So Consciousness can be likened to an eternal infinite lake, or ocean, in which ripples arise, abide and subside leaving It unchanged. All of this movement is seen by Awareness which is a facet of Consciousness Itself, but which is ever unmoving aware of the movements occurring within it. For to be totally aware of everything occurring in any situation one has to be totally still ... and it is in contrast to this stillness that the 'ripples' (thoughts, mental images and sensations in our case) can be seen – that is one becomes aware of them.

One - Relaxing into Awareness of Awareness

Two simple methods (among many) for relaxing into 'awareness of Awareness' - a practice which I advise those who have had an awakening, by becoming aware of (and identified with) Awareness, to undertake thrice daily. For a more 'freestyle method' see chapter twenty four - A *Morning Contemplation/Relaxation.*

I have often said that I recommend relaxing into 'awareness of Awareness' for at least 20 minutes three times a day and for those of you who find this hard here is a straightforward format for doing this.

1/ Locate yourself somewhere where there will be as little (hopefully no) outside disturbance whatsoever, deactivate your phone and turn off any electronic sound source. Ensure that any other residents will not disturb you. Sit or lie in this most comfortable position you can find, preferably with a straight spine, but this is not compulsory. The important thing is that there should be no physical discomfort.

2/ Maintain the intention to be 'aware of Awareness' throughout the practice and settle back into the support that the furnishing(s) provides. Relax your body as much as you can by inhaling deeply and mentally repeating 'relax' as you inhale/exhale[4] and feeling the muscles letting go as you do this. Repeat this until you feel no more physical letting go and relaxation occurring. You can do the practice with eyes open or closed, whichever you prefer, although there will probably be less distractions with them closed.

3/ Notice simply that you are aware of thoughts and sensations and thus Awareness is already present. This noticing (becoming aware) of

---

[4] Breathing should be done through the nose where possible. I actually repeat 're' on the inhalation and 'lax' on the exhalation, later similarly 'let' ... then 'go', and finally 'nothing' .. 'to do'. So we get 're ... lax', 'let ... go', and 'nothing ... to do' with the inhalation/exhalation. I find this method to be very relaxing and soothing.

Awareness is the 'awareness of Awareness' that is to be maintained (or returned to when overlooked) throughout the practice.

4/ Whilst maintaining this (awareness of Awareness) mentally repeat 'let go ... let go ... let go' allowing all of your thought streams to effortlessly subside as you do this. Continue this for some time and notice that the mind becomes quieter and quieter. Do not worry if this does not occur as Awareness (of these 'streams') is always present, otherwise you would not know they were there. This realization is also becoming 'aware of Awareness' ... which is the aim of the practice!

5/ As Awareness is obviously already present there is nothing to achieve, for how can you achieve what is already the case. Just recognize (become aware of) this and let go of any effort to achieve anything, as in this practice there is nothing to achieve! Just relax even more deeply, as you let all efforting go, by mentally repeating 'relax ... no effort ...relax ... no effort ... relax ... relax ... relax ...' until no more relaxation is occurring. Then repeat step 4 before moving on to the next step.

6/ Also you can let go of all searching and seeking for it is apparent that Awareness is always here (and now!) and thus need not be found ... for it can never be lost(!) ... just overlooked to our cost. If you doubt this just ask yourself whether there has ever been a time when you are (were) aware that Awareness was not present? This question is obviously an oxymoron that can never be answered in the positive. Even whilst asleep (when you could not ask this) Awareness is always present, although in abeyance, ready to notice any dreams or physical sensations that become strong enough to wake one up. So, having seen this you can relax even more deeply as the effort involved with seeking can be relinquished by mentally repeating 'relax … nothing to find … relax … nothing to find … relax … nothing to find' until no deeper relaxation takes place'. Then repeat step 4 before moving on to the next step.

7/ Finally realize that all longing for and acquiring of liberation (enlightenment, nirvana, freedom, moksha etc.) can be let go, for becoming 'aware of' and identifying with Awareness is this. Thus you do not need to long for, or acquire, that which you already have (**and are**!)… So, having seen this you can relax even more deeply as the effort involved with longing and acquiring can be relinquished by mentally repeating 'relax … nothing to desire … relax … nothing to get … relax … nothing to desire … relax … nothing to get' until no deeper relaxation takes place. Then repeat step 4 informed by the knowing that there is nothing to achieve, find, desire or acquire … and thus all effort to 'do' or 'be' anything can be released.

8/ As you breathe in and out with the mental repetition notice the 'gaps' that occur between the inhalation and exhalation and vice-versa. In these gaps there is no 'noise', silence, nothingness and it is in contrast to this that the mental repetition is noticed. This nothingness is a property of Awareness – Consciousness at rest, for all 'things' are manifestations of cosmic energy – Consciousness in motion. So as you repeat 're … lax …re …lax …re …lax …' and so on be aware of the 'sounds' in the mind and also the 'silences' (gaps) in which they occur.

9/ Continue this relaxing into 'awareness of Awareness', letting go of all effort and allowing the mind to quieten more and more, or not as the case may be! At all events thoughts and sensations are to be seen as objects coming and going in Awareness, and the fact that you are aware of them proves that Awareness is already (and always) present. When you decide to end this practice come out of it slowly by becoming totally aware of all your surroundings and strengthen its power by returning to the effortless 'awareness of Awareness' at frequent periods throughout the day.

Relaxing into Awareness of Awareness – Two

Another 'way' of relaxing into 'awareness of Awareness' occurs when the mind is untroubled, and one-pointed, before entering the 'practice'. This occurs when, as soon as the mind is directed towards (becomes aware of) Awareness itself, it is seen to be obviously the case that Awareness is already, and always, present. This is becoming aware of the serene 'lake of Awareness' and occurs by noticing the 'ripples' (thoughts/feelings/sensations) which reveal the 'lake' in which they occur.

When this is starkly 'seen' then the knowing that the 'lake' is ever present, and that at the deepest level one is that lake (rather than the ripples), is enough to produce profound peace and relaxation. For Awareness itself, Consciousness at rest, is by definition still and silent – always at peace. This is the case even when the mind cannot experience that the lake is present, for there are no ripples, but still knows (and is profoundly quietened by this 'knowing') of Its presence. In this case there is no need to 'do' anything with the mind which is held in abeyance and just sees that the ripples arise and subside in the lake without following, or buying into, any of them.

Thus the mind remains completely still (untroubled – at peace), even as the occasional thought passes through it, in resonance with the stillness of the lake in which it 'knows' that it exists. As this peace deepens the number of thoughts lessens and lessens until one enters a 'timeless zone' for time is apparent by the 'events' occurring in it and when there is absolutely nothing happening (at all!) then there is no awareness of time. So be warned that, not only does one 'lose oneself' (hallelujah!) in this 'practice', but that one also 'loses (knowledge of the passing of) time[5]' and so when 'one' (in this case the mind) emerges from this

---

[5] Time just being a man made concept to provide the mind with a framework in which to see (and 'manage') the flow of ephemeral events.

'awareness of Awareness' do not be surprised to find that it's much later than you think.

So this gives two 'ways' of relaxing into this knowing, one when the mind is already relaxed and another when the mind is in its usual busy mode. For a third see the last chapter which is a contemplation that occurred one morning when the mind was deluged by a seemingly unstoppable torrent of thoughts and mental images. I hope that these three will enhance 'the picture' of this practice for you, the reader.

Two – Experience and Response in Awareness

A discussion on the subject of the mechanism of our moment to moment experience and the response that this engenders.

Our moment to moment experience and the response that this engenders can be modelled as travelling through seven 'layers', three of which can be regarded as 'input', the fundamental layer of Awareness and then three which can be regarded as 'output'. The input layers are those through which the world is 'experienced', the fundamental layer is the constant conscious subjective presence which 'sees' this input, or where this input is 'displayed', and the output layers are those through which the mind processes the 'input' and then acts (or not) on its determinations. This is like a 'well' in which the input layers constitute a ladder on one wall, the fundamental layer the bottom and the output layers a ladder on the opposite wall.

The first outer layer is the so called physical reality of the manifest world, the top rung of both 'ladders'. This is detected by the mind/body as sense impressions/mental activity and this detection constitutes the second rung of the input layer. These detections are then processed by the brain and this processing is the third rung before the results are displayed in Awareness – that is to say that there is Awareness of them. This constitutes the input section – experience itself.

The mind is always scanning the 'screen' of Awareness checking the input (or 'display') for results to process. When it notices and focuses on any of these this is the third rung of the output, which we normally denote by saying "I became 'aware' of ..." Note that this is a limited incidence of Awareness itself, limited by the mind and its range. The mind then 'reprocesses' that which it has noticed and formulates a response to this, which is the second rung of the output. It is at this level that thoughts/mental images occur as they are not 'detectable' at the top-level (i.e. by the senses). The resulting action, or not, of this response then occurs in the physical reality of the manifest world, back at the top rung.

In this analogy Awareness, the bottom layer is the 'ground of being' which is common to both the experiential and the responsive layers. These latter two are in the realm of 'objects' and are thus in motion, as all matter is synonymous with energy and thus in motion. Awareness is a subjective presence which is still - displaying all that occurs in it, in the same way that a lake must be still to give an accurate reflection of its surroundings. The well is Consciousness Itself, Awareness when at rest and Cosmic Energy when (manifesting) in motion.

When consulting the schematic below follow the 'rungs' down to 'The Ground' and then those up from 'The Ground'.

Input - Experience

(Going Down)

'Rung' 1: Physical detectable (by the senses) 'reality'.
'Rung' 2: Detections by the body/mind ...Sense impressions/mental activity.

'Rung' 3:   Processing of these detections by the brain

'The Ground', Consciousness at rest, where the results of the brain's processing are displayed   on the 'Screen' of Pure Awareness. All of the 'rungs' are manifestations of Cosmic Energy – Consciousness in motion.

Output – Response

(Coming up)

'Rung' 3: Noticing, becoming 'aware' of, some of the results on the 'screen' of Pure Awareness.

'Rung' 2:   Mental reprocessing of what has been noticed

…Thoughts/mental images resulting.

'Rung' 1:   Actions occurring as a result in the physical 'reality'.

Both occurrences of 'rung 2' are fed into the input side of 'rung 3', thus appearing in the 'ground' of Awareness where they are noticed, resulting in a 'train of thought', which may or may not cause an action on the physical level.

Naturally, identification is the key to the final 'result' (response or reaction) to one's experience of the physical 'reality'. If one is identified with the second/third 'rungs' – mind/body, as a separate object in a world of such – then the mental reprocessing will be highly coloured by this, as it will be filtered through the screen of opinions, preferences, self-interest, self-image, and so on. This could well result in inappropriate actions, resulting in reactions rather than responses, which could produce unnecessary suffering for ourselves and (seeming) 'others'.

Whereas, if one is identified as 'The Ground' – with Consciousness Itself- then our body/minds are seen to be expressions and instruments of This. In this there is no separation and the mental reprocessing is unfiltered as the results, that are noticed on the 'screen' of Awareness, are seen 'as they are' and not through the filter of an imaginary 'separate self'. This results in spontaneous responses to our experiences rather than reactions, avoiding the unpleasant side-effects given above.

Becoming 'aware of Awareness' occurs when the mind is looking at the 'screen of Awareness' (as it always is) and notices the 'screen' Itself rather than anything occurring on it. This cannot be 'seen' in the same

6 By definition Awareness is Consciousness at rest and thus nothingness, for all 'things' are composed of cosmic energy and thus in motion.

way that the objects are displayed, but it can be truly known to be present otherwise there could be no Awareness of these objects. In fact it is the 'nothingness[6]' relative to which 'things' can be known and it is by the appearance of these 'things' within it that it can be known to be present. In the same way that you cannot see a lake which is absolutely still, reflecting its environment and stretching to the horizon, but when a stone is thrown into it the ripples reveals its presence.

Once one is truly 'aware of' (sees) the existence of this 'screen of Awareness' then this can be investigated to determine its properties, for more on this see step 9[7] onwards from the appendix 'Investigation of Experience'.

---

[7] The first eight steps are a process for revealing that, at the deepest level, **<u>we are this Awareness</u>**.

Three – A Modern Fix For Misidentification

A modern fix for misidentification based on the 'switching of users' when logged on to a computer.

.

About ten years ago I discovered an easy way to 'fix' a computer which has slowed down due to years of miscellaneous file accumulation and other rubbish caused by mis-use. This has ramifications for 'fixing' the mind which has become less efficient due to accumulation of memories, worries and the development of neuroses. The standard method for fixing a computer is to reformat the hard disc and then reload the operating system, all of the programs that were installed, and personal files/music/pictures etc. that have been saved. However, a much quicker and easier method is to go to the Control Panel, select 'Users' and create a new user as an 'Administrator'. Then one saves all personal information that one wishes to retain[8] and (still in 'Users') deletes one's old identity, after logging off and logging on with the identity of the newly created 'user'. Windows will ask you whether you wish to delete all of the files pertaining to the old 'identity' to which you should answer 'yes', which will remove all of the garbage that has been accumulated over the years that one has used the system.

This will virtually restore the system to its original pristine condition but with the added advantage that the operating system remains intact and all of the various programs that have been installed, and updated, over the many years are still available. Now you just reload all of your personal files/music/pictures etc. and there you are ... a very quick and simple fix. I have done this to many machines with stunning results and it's a very good party trick if you visit a friend who complains that

---

[8] Don't forget your bookmarked internet sites as these will be lost during the process.

their computer has become very slow and is tempted to buy a new one. It's also a great way to fix a second-hand computer that appears to be somewhat tardy...

Now with regard to the mind it would indeed be wonderful if one could adopt a similar procedure and with some modifications this is indeed possible! Obviously the radical 'disc reformat' method could not be used for this would virtually require physical death and reincarnation into a body with a new brain. Even in this case (if reincarnation is in fact possible) it is posited that one carries much mental 'crap' over into the new life and so this would not actually fix the problem. However, the creation of a new 'user' and then 'logging in' with this new identity is indeed possible. Now it is true that there is no easy method to delete the old identity but as long as one stays 'logged in' as the new identity then the neuroses and worries of the old one lose their weight as they are seen to not pertain to the present one ...

This is easy to do by investigating one's moment to moment experience, see the appendix, which reveals that deeper than the body/mind (thoughts/feelings/mental images and sensations) is a deeper level of 'Pure Awareness'. This is the constant conscious subjective presence that we all essentially 'are' in which the flow of objects, just mentioned, takes place and by which these 'objects' are seen. When one identifies with (as) This new 'user', that one has just discovered, then one no longer identifies with (or as) this ephemeral flow (which are experienced as the body/mind) and thus they lose their weight. In this peace is the natural condition as Pure Awareness (Consciousness at rest) is always still, witnessing the slightest movements occurring within it, and silent, witnessing the smallest sounds ...

As soon as any worries or neuroses occur then, if identified with, they produce mental suffering which is a sure sign that one has re-identified with the original 'user' (body/mind). The simple solution to this is to 'log off' and 'log on' as the newly discovered identity Pure Awareness, and this is achieved by reinvestigation of this actual moment (of experience) as given in the appendix. When adept at this the simple seeing that one is aware of these worries/neuroses, and that these are objects appearing in this Awareness that one **is,** will suffice. This is an ongoing process as we have misidentified for countless years and so are liable to do so again at any minute until established in the new identity. However, this is not a cause for concern for every time we have to reinvestigate (log-off and then log-on) this produces peace and joy as all of the burdens pertaining to the old identity are lifted ... The more often we carry out the investigation, and see the cogency of this, the more we become established in our new essential identity and the less often we will slip back into misidentification.

After the initial discovery that one **is** Pure Awareness, at the deepest level, I recommend that one carries out the full investigation, and relaxes into 'awareness of Awareness', three times a day. The longer this is maintained the deeper the establishment will become until this procedure is transcended as it is no longer necessary, but this will not be the case until the flip-flopping between the two 'users' (identities) has ceased. You will know that this has occurred when the worries and neuroses of the old 'user' no longer affect you, even if they continue to 'come up'… Also all existential angst and needless mental suffering will cease. This does indeed slowly re-format the mind as due to neuro-plasticity new pathways are forged in the brain and the old ones (samskaras) fall into disuse due to losing their over-riding importance as to saying anything about what we truly **are.**

Four – Loyalty and Awakening

Discusses the need to be loyal, or true, to Awakening in order to remain 'awake'.

Concerning 'The Philosophy of Loyalty' by Josiah Royce:

> He believed that we all seek a cause beyond ourselves … and dedication to this cause he called loyalty. He regarded it as the opposite of individualism. The individualist puts self-interest first, seeing his own pain, pleasure and existence as his greatest concern. For an individualist loyalty to causes that have nothing to do with self-interest seems strange. When such loyalty encourages self-sacrifice, it can even be alarming – a mistaken and irrational tendency.

> In fact he argued human beings *need* loyalty. It does not necessarily produce happiness, and can even be painful, but we all require devotion to something more than ourselves for life to be endurable. Without it, we have only our desires to guide us, and they are fleeting, capricious and insatiable. They provide, ultimately, only torment …[9]

Loyalty and dedication are perfect ways to describe what is needed once one has glimpsed one's true essence Pure Awareness. One needs to stay true to this glimpse and continue the investigation until one has really 'seen' that This is what one actually is at the core, beneath the surface layer of body/mind (thoughts, mental images, feelings and sensations).

---

[9] Gawande Atul, *Being Mortal*, 2014, London, p.126

When one stays loyal to this realization one can see that this is true of so-called 'others' and that we share the same essence expressing Itself in different ways. In this giving their interests the same (or even more) weight as our own becomes natural, for there is no separation. Before this occurs it may seem somewhat alarming due to our many years of putting our own interests first, but the seeing of 'oneness' means that does not seem irrational.

This loyalty, or you could call it dedication, means staying alert to the arising of misidentification, normally as the body/mind. For when this occurs we have once again identified ourself, and others, as separate objects in a universe of such. In this state self-interest tends to become paramount and the interests of others secondary. This always produces unnecessary mental suffering for ourself, and possibly others, which should be used as 'dharma bell' (wake up call) to the fact that we have fallen asleep again.

Then we need to reinvestigate and discover that we are the Pure Awareness that seeming objects occur in … see the appendix. In fact I recommend that one carries out this investigation at least three times daily until one is established in this realization. This process is dedication to That and the outcomes of this such as universal love, compassion, non-clinging etc., occur naturally if one stays loyal to this true Self-recognition. For without this indeed: 'we have only our desires to guide us, and they are fleeting, capricious and insatiable. They provide, ultimately, only torment ...' And this torment is the clue that misidentification has reoccurred.

Dedication is where Jnana (the path of knowledge) and Bhakti (that of devotion) meet, for both require the surrendering of the 'small self', the difference being in the method employed to achieve this. The former is by direct seeing that the 'small self' is an illusion for in essence we are Pure Awareness. Whereas, the latter uses self abasement and glorification of the Ishta (form that is worshipped) to achieve self-surrender.

Loyalty also means trusting one's direct seeing and not seeking other paths when doubts occur. For although other paths may offer tempting powers, or experiences, these are all just ephemeral manifestations occurring within the Pure Awareness that we are. So when doubts occur reinvestigation, which reveals that we are That, is the key ... the pathless path - for no movement (or improvement) is required!

Five – Judgement and Misidentification

A discussion about judging 'others' and how this requires for the 'judge' to be misidentified for this to occur.

I recently noticed this comment about my conscioustv interview on utube, 'Beyond The Separate Self'. Bear in mind that I was somewhat over my usual weight due to extended holidaying with friends, and family, and their abundant hospitality, but I was certainly not anywhere near 'obese':

Watching This 2 days ago

> I think there is a contradiction with spiritual people. They appear passively detached and so you can remain addicted to a drug, overweight and never know the reason why. Colin Drake for example, is overweight, which means despite constant mental awareness he doesn't know which foods are best suited to his body. Obesity is a normal way of life, you may saying to you yourself. BUT IS IT? We are the only species (apart from animals we have domesticated) on the entire planet that suffer from obesity. So all is has achieved is a certain level of detachment. There is no sign of intelligence working these issues out and fixing them.

Here is my reply, just to put the record straight:

Colin Drake 1 day ago
+Watching This

Yesterday's breakfast was home-made muesli with yoghurt, banana and pear followed by half a piece of toast of home-baked wholemeal bread with homemade marmalade. Lunch was a piece of the same toast with avocado and dinner was a small fresh salmon steak with steamed potatoes, broccoli and carrots. This is fairly indicative of our daily diet. Since coming to live (in1982) on a ten acre run-down macadamia plantation and building a pottery I have worked physically pretty hard. Due to this I have become pretty 'solid' in fact my sons say I am built 'like a tank'! But that has not stopped me from doing my 15 minute morning yoga session every day (plus meditation and yoga-nidra) and I am still very healthy and supple, not bad for a 67 year old with no health problems at all.

The interview was conducted at the end of an extended holiday staying with family and friends with whom I (we) had shared many a happy copious meal complete with the odd glass of wine. So due to this overindulgence I was somewhat 'bursting at the seams' by the time I was interviewed! However, I knew this would not be a problem for when we got home I underwent a three day fast which shrunk my stomach. The result of which is that eating less, and the amazingly healthy diet containing many home-grown fruit and vegetables, has solved the problem and now, happily, all of my clothes fit me again. If you doubt my energy levels just re-watch the interview and note the amount of enthusiasm displayed ... in fact I am committed to aiding as many people as I can to awaken!

So you can see that the judgement made was based on insufficient information, as I certainly do know which foods are best for my body and I also used my intelligence to correct the problem when I returned! Which made me ponder why some people are so ready to negatively judge others at the risk of appearing ridiculous when the full facts are known. It seems to me that this is caused by the age old problem of identifying oneself, and others, as a separate object in a world of such. For in the above example the viewer has made a judgement about my (lack of) intelligence purely by the fact that my body was slightly overweight without taking any account of what was being said!

Actually the judging mind will always judge itself as harshly as others, unless it uses judging others as a strategy to avoid looking at itself. Such judgements are always of the body/mind, overlooking that which is at the core of each being, the constant conscious subjective presence, and so are of no use in the quest for self-realization by self-inquiry. Gangaji famously said that if you want to 'improve', or change, your personality you had better do it before you 'wake up'; for after 'awakening' you won't care about it! When you look at the seemingly bizarre behaviour (and appearance) of many awakened beings it is obvious that there is no 'model' for the body, behaviour, or personality, of such a being; and to form negative judgements based on these is to overlook That which they are pointing to - the essence of who (or what) we are.

At all events this type of analysis of oneself, and others, can only occur when there is objectification, for more on this see 'Analysis – The Disease not The Cure' in *Awareness of Awareness – The Open Way.* For, when one sees that the deepest level of being is Pure Awareness, one sees oneself and 'others' as That which lacks nothing and is always pure and pristine. To achieve this I have always stressed investigation of moment-to-moment experience which reveals that beneath thoughts/sensations/feelings/emotions (fleeting objects) is Awareness, otherwise we would be unaware of them! This is the constant (check for yourself to see if this is ever not present* ...)[10], conscious (by definition), subjective (the seer of the previously mentioned objects), changeless presence* (not a thing, but always here all the same) which has been (with) you ever since you were born. Whereas, the fleeting objects (everything experienced in, and by, the body/mind) are ephemeral and ever changing. So what (or who) are you within this??

---

[10] Even during sleep there is awareness of dreams and sensations, such that if a sensation becomes strong enough it will wake one up. There also seems to be some awareness of the quality of the sleep in that we can report on this the next morning …

60

Even memory is ever-changing and unreliable, in fact the only constant element in all of this is the Awareness, and as I am sure that you feel that you have constantly been present (and witnessed) your entire life the only logical conclusion can be that you are this Awareness!!

Please consider this carefully ... I can assure you that once you are truly convinced that Awareness is your essential being then identifying with (and as) this becomes (almost) second nature. When this occurs unnecessary mental suffering and judgements, caused by misidentification, are negated.

This Awareness (Consciousness at rest) is That in which all manifestation (cosmic energy -Consciousness in motion) arises abides and subsides. For all movement arises in (and from) stillness, exists in (and is known relative to) that stillness, and finally returns to stillness. Thus Awareness is pure for it is untainted by the ephemeral movements occurring in It, pristine for these movements cannot degrade It, and radiant for they are 'seen' by Its 'light'.

When one sees that this is That which we are at the deepest level then negative judgements drop away as That is ever pure and pristine. Also one sees all 'others' as That, and their body/minds as ephemeral expressions and instruments of That.

It is interesting to note that extensive research done on NDEs (near death experiences) has revealed that the spiritual beings that are encountered never exhibit any negative judgements and that the only occurrences of these are in the form of self-judgement. Such self-judging can only occur when one is misidentified as a separate object, for it is the ephemeral aspects of one's being that are judged – the body/mind – and not the fundamental eternal essence.

Six – Awakening is For All

Following on from the previous chapter this insists that 'awakening' is available to all and not restricted to a 'chosen' few.

Here is a comment, taken from his final email to me, by one of my 'readers', who had written rave reviews of my books, before he unsubscribed himself from my email group:

> I think there is a great distinction between being 'awake' for some of the time and 'enlightenment'. I would be very wary myself of confusing the two because one could be awake and still dominated by the ego. I think anyone that has spent ten minutes listening to Ram Das can clearly tell he is not enlightened. Osho, who I trust more that most, confirms as much in one of his discourses. He also believed that Alan Watts was not enlightened either. I agree with him on that point too. The only two people I have found to be genuinely enlightened so far are Osho and Gangaji. The rest that I have seen are either deluding themselves or deluding their readers.

This shows confused thinking as one cannot be awake and dominated by the ego, for the two are mutually exclusive! His comments about Ram Das and Alan Watts show that he is ego-centric for who is he to say? But the main problem is in the final comment; for if he is prepared to dismiss everyone, but the two he has mentioned, he limits the chances of his own (or anybody else's) awakening by assigning those who he thinks have achieved this to such a small and select group. Not only that but Osho was said by some to be addicted to nitrous oxide (laughing gas) and also collected Rolls Royces, whereas Gangaji used to get angry with her support staff and she also underwent cosmetic surgery to maintain a youthful 'look'; in addition she was obsessively particular about her accommodation and the set-up of her venues when on tour;. I know because I was the overall co-ordinator of her Byron Bay satsangs in 1999 and the manual I was given to work with was about two inches thick. In fact I often said that organising her event was like producing 'Ben Hur'!

But none of this matters if the teachings that these beings gave helped people to awaken, for if this is the case then their body-type, behaviour and life-style are totally irrelevant. There is no model for the character, actions and idiosyncrasies of an awakened being. 'The proof of the pudding is in the eating' as they say and in Gangaji's case I can report that she helped many to awaken. I was at a seven day silent retreat with her in 1996 and heard many genuine first-hand accounts by participants who had awakened due to her pointings and their willingness to 'let go'. Whether these awakenings were permanent or temporary I cannot say but they were certainly totally credible as they were recounted. In my case I had my first genuine awakening on that retreat and have fostered this ever since with repeated self-inquiry and contemplation.

Since then I have written seven books on awakening and have received many encouraging emails from readers who have awakened themselves by following my pointers and conducting their own investigations. I am sure that none of these would have achieved this if they believed that there were only a small select group who were enlightened. With regard to this: enlightenment and awakening are the same thing but the former is only the case where the latter is constant, another thing that my earlier correspondent was confused about. If one thinks that there are only a few beings on the planet who have awakened then one would surmise that one's own chances of joining this rare group are pretty slim. Whereas Gangaji and Osho both disagreed with this and spent much time promoting the ease of awakening. Also Papaji (Gangaji's guru) famously said that 'the final obstacle (to awakening) is believing that there is an obstacle' and Sri Ramana Maharshi (his guru) went even further by saying that awakening was easy. Although he did qualify that by saying 'that then the work begins', which means that one has to establish the first awakening by repeated self-inquiry until one is permanently awake.

And the only one who can tell if one is awake is oneself, any judgement made by another is liable to be faulty as all such judgements are based on misidentification of the 'judge' and the 'other' that they are judging. Also when one discovers the Pure Awareness (in which our thoughts and sensations arise, abide, are spied and subside), which we are at the deepest level, then negative judgements drop away as That is ever pure and pristine. To recognize the ease of this, by investigation of one's moment to moment experience, see the appendix. Then one sees all 'others' as That, and their body/minds as ephemeral expressions and instruments of That. Thus one realizes that all are essentially the same 'One' and this reinforces one's understanding of the 'ease of awakening', making one more liable to give credence to the reports of awakening given by those that we encounter.

His email also contained other comments which showed that he had misinterpreted much of what I had written. The whole email exchange left me somewhat sad that someone who had read, and lauded, my books could have come to the conclusions he did. Here is my final reply to him;

With acknowledgements to Rumi:

I have no longing except for the One,
When a wind of personal reaction comes,
I do not go along with it

There are many winds full of anger,
And lust and greed. They move the rubbish
Around, but the solid mountains of our true nature
Stays where it's always been.

There's nothing now
Except the divine qualities,
Come through the opening into me.

Your misinterpretation was better than any reverence,

Because in this moment I am you and you are me.

I give you this open heart as God gives gifts:

The negativity of your message has become,

The honey of friendship.

The personal reaction, that your last message evoked, was one of my ineptitude that allowed my writings and emails to be so misinterpreted. I always try to write with clarity, consistency and honesty but your last message showed me how much I have failed. It just shows how slippery words can be! Truly as the 'Tao Te Ching' says 'the Tao that can be spoken is not the Tao'! Love, Colin

Seven – Lack of Interest in Awakening

Discusses why most people are not interested in 'awakening'.

Most people are not interested in awakening for they cannot countenance the fact that they are asleep; that is to say that they are identified as a separate object in a universe of such and, more pertinently, with their self image. As awakening is to realize that this self-image is an imaginary construct and that beyond this one **is** the constant conscious subjective presence (Pure Awareness) which 'sees' this self-image, then whilst one feels that one **is** this self-image one cannot possibly understand the concept of awakening. In which case any consideration, or discussion, of 'awakening' is impossible as one imagines that one is already awake!

This is why I stress self-identity, discovering the essence of one's being, as the best way to overcome needless mental anxiety and suffering. This is easily achieved by investigating one's own moment-to-moment experience, see the appendix, and then honouring what is discovered by repeating the investigation whenever misidentification reoccurs; for this will always produce suffering for oneself, and possibly 'others'. This should be used as a sign that one is back at the surface level of thoughts and sensations and used as a trigger to resume the investigation which reveals the deeper level of Pure Awareness that we all share, and are.

Once this discovery has taken place one can see that identification with the surface level entails being asleep, for then one is tossed by the storm of ever changing flow of ephemeral objects which we experience as thoughts (including mental images), sensations and 'feelings' which are a combination of these. Whereas, at the deeper level there is only peace, for Awareness is always silent - witnessing the smallest sound and thought, and still - witnessing the slightest movement of body or mind. Within this thoughts and sensations come and go leaving it unaffected, so identification with this Awareness means that one is also fundamentally untroubled by these. This in turn means that the mind is quieter and thus more able to solve problems that come up, without the background programs, of (small) self-concern and self-interest, running. These programs are like a continual dream state that stop one from seeing 'what is' as everything that is encountered is viewed through the distorting filter of self-image. Thus when this is removed it truly feels like one has awakened from a bad dream.

However, when one is in the dream one is only aware of this when this is lucid dreaming, that is when one is aware that one is dreaming during the dream itself. So the first task in trying to aid others to awaken is to point out that they are in fact 'asleep', and that they're living a 'dream' (identified as a separate object in a world of such) from which they can escape by 'awakening'. It is only when this is realized that any interest, or belief, in the possibility of such 'awakening' takes place. Until this takes place most people will not be interested in, or consider, the whole subject and will tend to think that those who are interested in this are themselves deluded!

One of the easiest ways I find to introduce this subject, to someone who seems open to the idea, is to point to the fact that we all share the same 'life-force'. This seems to be fairly readily acceptable and from there it's a short step to naming this 'Consciousness' and from this to introduce the concept of Awareness. Then by conducting the first few steps of the investigation into direct experience, mentioned above and given in full in the appendix, most people readily see that this Awareness is the deeper level of being which 'sees' (is aware of) thoughts and sensations (body/mind). Following from this - seeing that, at this deeper level, one **is** Awareness is but another small step and a cogent conclusion based on the evidence just presented above.

Eight – The Omnipresent/Omniscience Paradox

This chapter considers the paradox that 'awakening' occurs by identifying with Pure Awareness, which is omnipresent and omniscient, but that this does not lead to personal omnipresence and omniscience.

Here is an email exchange and discussion regarding omnipresence and the misconception that self-realization automatically leads to one personally experiencing this. That is to say how realizing the omnipresent Self does not necessarily lead to personal omniscience (the mind having access to everything that exists in Consciousness). This is a paradox, as realizing that one is the Self (Consciousness) that is the essence of all - 'the omnipresent, omniscient, ocean in which all things arise, abide and subside'- it would be natural to assume that one would also exhibit these properties.

Hello

I have got your email from Eleonora from conscious.tv

I have some doubts about nonduality, Self realisation, enlightenment etc.

Please try to explain as possible as you can.

My point in this case (Self Realization, God Realization or Enlightenment) is

This state is Omnipresent. Ok.

for ex. if I am a God Realised person I am living in you too, right,

So I should know your past and I must feel when your body hurt.

Then I can say I am in you. Otherwise I am not Omnipresent.

But those people who claim Self Realised don't have these capability.

They say always we are in the essence of all being.

Essence I think all qualities should come in a fine form.

Thank you Colinj

Dear XXXX, Good to hear from you, see my replies, in italics, to your points below:

My point in this case (Self Realization, God Realization or Enlightenment) is

This state is Omnipresent. Ok.

Self Realization is not a state. It is realizing the Self, which is to say discovering the essence that lies at the centre of, in fact constitutes, each being and all things. Then living from this realization that Awareness, Consciousness at rest, is this essence in which all things which consist of cosmic energy (Consciousness in motion) arise, abide and subside.

for ex. if I am a God Realised person I am living in you too, right,

The mind/body is an ephemeral expression of this Consciousness and is unique in the same way that a wave on the ocean is unique but is still of the same essence (water), and not separate from, the ocean. The essential 'I' (Consciousness) is the same in each of us but our mind/bodies are seemingly distinct in the same way as the wave on (in) the ocean.

So I should know your past and I must feel when your body hurt.

No, for this knowing and feeling is distinct to each mind/body.

Then I can say I am in you. Otherwise I am not Omnipresent.

Consciousness is Omnipresent, in the same way that water is omnipresent in the ocean, and is (in) all, but the ephemeral expressions are temporarily unique, as are waves of the ocean.

But those people who claim Self Realised don't have this capability.

Self realised people have realised the Self, the essence, Awareness (Consciousness at rest) – but their experiences (thoughts, mental images and sensations) are unique to each mind/body, it is the Awareness that is common to all. Each mind (generally) only has access to the flow of thoughts, mental images and sensations that appear on the screen of Awareness, occurring in that mind/body. Rather like the RAM of a computer, each program only has access to that portion in which it and its buffer reside and work, but the RAM is a contiguous whole.

They say always we are in the essence of all being.

Consciousness, of which we are fleeting manifestations, is the essence of all being.
For more on this please watch my interview on conscioustv, or read any of my books – see the attachment. Then if you have more questions I will be happy to answer them, Love, Colin

Essence I think all qualities should come in a fine for
Thank you Colinj

I understood so, it is like an Orange and its Juice.

Orange has form and inside we can see many other layers.

In Orange Juice we get the Essence of Orange , so everything is in it, but no form.

Am I right?

Yes, the essence is the never-changing within which the form(s), the ever-changing, come and go.

And yet, as I wrote in a previous article, as we are in essence Awareness Itself it could be theoretically possible that one could access everything that appears in Consciousness ... There is some evidence for this in the reports of the experiences of some famous enlightened beings. Sri Ramakrishna was said to be able to read minds, The Buddha was said to have knowledge of his previous incarnations, Jesus was purported to have many powers including knowing what was in his disciple minds and so on ...

There are also many instances of mystics saying things like 'I am the omnipresent, omniscient, One in whom all things arise, abide and subside', but whether this means that any of them actually experienced personal omniscience (their mind being able to see everything in Consciousness) is debatable. Indeed I am one of these, for by my own experiences and investigations, see the appendix and 'Spiritual Experience' in Beyond The Separate Self, I could well make the same statement. But this would just mean that I have realised the essence, Pure Awareness (Consciousness at rest), which is at the centre of my (and all) being to which the statement applies; and that by further investigations/contemplations I have come to realise the validity of each word in it. Needless to say I do not exhibit personal omniscience and the only hint of this is in the intuitions that arise during my 'practice' and spontaneously as I answer questions or write articles.

However, consider 'Morphic Resonance' the theory that Rupert Sheldrake developed to explain formative causation where organisms seemed to have information, pertinent to the activity in which they were engaged, which they had not necessarily independently accessed. That is to say that the information was previously in existence (discovered by other organisms of the same type) and this made it much more readily accessible. For more on this see http://www.iawaketechnologies.com/morphic-resonance where there are listed seven scientific studies which support the theory.

This is also supported by almost simultaneous major discoveries. In 1922, William Ogburn and Dorothy Thomas discovered 148 scientific discoveries that fit a pattern referred to by science historians as multiples. A multiple is said to occur when a particular scientific discovery is found to have emerged in multiple geographic locations either simultaneously or within the same time period, but independently of each other. These observations, along with many other studies, discoveries and even spiritual texts not mentioned here, paint the picture of a shared informational field to which we all subtly entrain. This refined and often unconscious or intuitive mutual resonance— between field and organism—appears to help us cognize the world in which we live.[11]

---

[11] http://www.iawaketechnologies.com/morphic-resonance

Nine – Dealing With Self Hatred

A method for dealing with self hatred and discusses how this is a prime indicator of misidentification.

.

Here is an email exchange regarding dealing with self-hatred. My comments are in italics.

Hi Colin,

I am working with your enquiries and am beginning to have some successes.

Furthermore, when taking attention back on ItSelf, to Awareness, there was on a few occasions an extraordinary sense of relief as well as a deep bliss. This has happened on the beach a few times and once even in the car. I think you'll agree that that is a pretty good start.

I am very glad to hear it and fully agree that it is a very good start. There is such a feeling of relief when one discovers that all of the rubbish that one has thought about oneself is just that ...rubbish! And therefore of no weight or validity. This lifts the great burden of imaginary 'small selfhood' and often leads to bliss, the bliss that becomes a natural 'ease of being' as one becomes accustomed to it.

However, self-hatred arrives on a daily basis - coming out of the blue - normally staying for many hours. It's marked by substantial stress, and generally causes a very poor night's sleep, as I am unable to fully turn it off.

Dealing With Self Hatred

Self-hatred is an interesting double misidentification for there is the imaginary self that one builds stories about leading to it being 'hated' and then there is the illusory one that 'hates' this imaginary one!! So my question is who are these 'ones'?? Also who is aware of this 'hate'? As soon as this old habit resurfaces this is the time to restart the investigation to answer these questions ... If you can achieve this there is no need to 'turn it off' just let it come and go in That which the investigation reveals.

There are no words associated with it at the time it takes hold, but when I do something that does not go exactly as expected, there will be a cursing of myself, and then I finally realise what is going on.

There might not be words but, as you have pointed out, there will always (eventually) be discomfort which should be used as the sign that misidentification has occurred thus requiring the investigation to recommence. Also, as I say in 'Beyond The Separate Self:

'

> *This (accepting 'what is') also means accepting our mistakes and not berating ourselves for them, for until we are totally identified with, and as, pure awareness, we will continue to make mistakes. Normal life is a mixture of correct decisions and mistakes and should be accepted as such. As we become more 'awake' we will make less mistakes, but until then we can always see any annoyance caused by our errors for what it is: just a mixture of*

fleeting thoughts and sensations. Once again, if one relaxes into the deeper level of pure awareness one will see that this is totally unaffected by anything occurring at the surface level of mind/body. At this deeper level each moment is enough, or perfect in itself, as awareness just witnesses 'what is' without ever seeking to change anything.

The other day I came across a passage by Rumi, something like "the exhaustion of self-hatred", possibly in one of your books. (a web search did not reveal anything)

The quote you are looking for is in the introduction to 'Awareness of Awareness – The Open Way':

> *Rumi described this (Awareness) as: 'the clear conscious core of your being, the same in ecstasy as in self-hating fatigue'. That is to say the Awareness in which the ecstasy or the self-hating fatigue appears. Now generally you would just be aware of, and affected by, the phenomenal state. If, however, you become aware of the Awareness in which this state is occurring and can fully identify with, and as, this Awareness then the state loses its power to affect your equanimity. For Awareness is always utterly still and silent, totally unaffected by whatever*

appears in it, in the same way that the sky is unaffected by the clouds that scud across it.

Which gives the clue to overcoming self-hatred by becoming aware of (and identifying with) Awareness, for in this case the self-hate may still arise (out of habit) but it is given no weight as an indicator of who (or what) you are and thus is just seen to be an old story that has not yet exhausted itself.

I would love to transcend this energetic turning on myself and I would appreciate any further advice that you may have. Warm regards, XXXX

Self-hatred is a classic symptom of misidentification, in fact one could argue that it is the major symptom, for others such as mental suffering are sometimes unavoidable and occasionally even occur to those who are awake. Once one has discovered that one is Pure Awareness, which is easy to do (see the appendix), one has discovered the true Self at the heart of all which is ever loveable ... in fact is love itself. So whenever self-hatred rears its ugly head this is a sure sign that misidentification is occurring and the investigation (of one's moment to moment experience) needs to resume revealing the constant conscious subjective presence - which is our fundamental innermost essence. In this way self-hatred becomes a tool to lead us back to correct identification, which itself entails the end of the problem. The more one becomes established in awakening – as Pure Awareness – the less this problem will occur until it finally peters out when misidentification ceases, but until then it need not be resisted (or 'bought into') just used a cue to reawaken!

To truly achieve this one must also 'give up the story' of who, or what, one thinks one is ... see chapter of this name in *Awakening and Beyond*.

Ten – Nonduality and The Trinity

A chapter that considers the Christian Trinity giving a non-dual interpretation of this.

Bede Griffiths, the well known Benedictine monk who founded a Christian 'ashram' in India, writes:

> When the source, the Father, begets himself, manifests himself, in the Son it makes this bond of love. The Holy Spirit is the love that flows between the Father and Son. This stream of love that flows between them is the Holy Spirit; and that [Father, Son and Holy Spirit] is the Trinity. The ultimate reality … is a communion of love and we are all called to participate in that communion. That is the end of human existence and Jesus realized in his person the communion with the Father and the Spirit. I think there's a fullness in this Christian Trinity, which you don't find elsewhere, but there are indications everywhere of it.[12]

This source is Consciousness at rest, Awareness - the constant conscious subjective presence, which manifests itself, creates the display of objects in the universe, by 'moving' or creating movements within itself. For all 'things' are composed of cosmic energy and thus in motion … In this there is 'no separation', for all is Consciousness, and love **is** 'no separation'.[13] Thus the source and

---

[12] Griffiths B., *On Retreat With Bede Griffiths*, 1997, London

[13] All motion arises from stillness, exists in a substratum of stillness, can be known relative to that stillness, and subsides back into stillness. The energy required for this comes from the limitless store of 'dark energy' available within

its manifestation exist in a unity of love, and these three (this trinity) is nondual … the ultimate reality. We all participate in this communion, whether we know it or not, as in essence we are Awareness (Consciousness at rest) using our unique body/mind as instruments to engage with, enjoy, know and love its manifestation. We also have the capacity to realize this through self-inquiry, contemplation, meditation etc. When this realization has taken place this leads to enjoying, knowing and loving the source itself which deepens the previously mentioned communion … that of Consciousness knowing itself in both modes – at rest as Awareness, and in motion as the manifestation.

The knowing of this is 'the end of human existence', that is to say self-realization, when one realizes that our human existence is

---

Consciousness, and it is to this store that energy returns when it is totally dissipated.

Consciousness at Rest and in Motion

The Source from which all things arise,

The Ground in which they all abide,

The Seer by which they are spied,

The Knower by which they're cognized,

The Enjoyer by which they are prized,

The Nothingness into which they subside,

When out of momentum … the end of the ride.

restricted to the body/mind and that our essential self (Awareness) transcends (and contains) this. Jesus certainly recognized this and achieved the full communion with Father and the Holy Spirit: 'as we are one' (John 17 v.11) and 'I and my Father are one' (John 10 v.30). There is indeed a fullness in this Christian Trinity and, although it may not be spelt out in the same way, you certainly do find it everywhere. For in reality there is no separation, as all is Consciousness, and thus no union is needed. The communion is 'experienced' when this is fully realized and all humans (and maybe other species or aliens ...) have the potential to do this. The only uniqueness of the Christian model of the Trinity is in the nomenclature used, that of the Father, Son and Holy Spirit. In non sectarian and nondual terms this becomes that of Consciousness at rest (the source), in motion (the manifestation) and the relationship between (awareness of) these, or love (no separation) between these.

Further Bede says:

> Only the Spirit can set us free from the psyche and all its passions, desires, fears, hopes and so on. Meditation is calming the psyche letting go of all thoughts and feelings and becoming simply aware of the Holy Spirit; and at that point the human spirit unites with the Spirit of God, and we are in communion with God. When we let the other thoughts and things go we become aware of this indwelling presence.[14]

We become free from the psyche when we stop identifying with the mind and identify with Pure Awareness … which is the Spirit. Meditation is becoming 'aware of Awareness (the Holy Spirit)' when we can let go of thoughts and feelings by seeing them for what they are – ephemeral objects appearing in Awareness. At that point the human spirit, our limited awareness – the mind's noticing, or focussing on, something - 'unites with' with the Spirit of God (Pure Awareness) by becoming aware of it. In this 'awareness of Awareness' there is no separation and thus full communion. By becoming aware of this constant, conscious, indwelling presence (Awareness) letting thoughts and other things (come and) go becomes easy; for we no longer identify with them but with (and as) this presence.

Bede continues:

> John Main said that to pray, to meditate is to share in the consciousness of Christ, and that is the stream of love which flows from the Father to the son, and from the Son to the Father in the Holy Spirit. That stream is always flowing from the Father. Jesus is always in communion with the Father, sharing the love and knowledge of the Father which flows out in the Holy Spirit and is communicated with us …

---

[14] *Ibid*, p.47

so that at that point of the Spirit we open upon the inner mystery of the Trinity. We come to the final absolute.[15]

We share in the consciousness of Christ by becoming 'aware of (and fully identifying with) Awareness' when we realize there is only oneness - 'I and my Father are one'. The stream of love which flows from Consciousness at rest (the Father) to its manifestation (of which the son, Christ, was a fully 'awakened' instance) is the awareness and realization of no-separation between the two 'modes' of Consciousness. This relationship in which Consciousness can know and love itself in both modes is, in Christian terms, the Holy Spirit. Jesus is always in communion with the Father for they 'are one' and there is never any separation between them. It is communicated with us when we realize that we are also essentially Consciousness at rest (Awareness) of which our body/minds are temporal expressions and instruments. So when we become 'aware of Awareness' the manifestation has become 'aware of' its source, and ground of being, and we have opened onto the mystery of the Trinity: Consciousness at rest becoming aware of (and knowing and loving) its manifestation – Consciousness in motion, and vice-versa! This is the final absolute.

---

[15] *Ibid*, p.47

Eleven – On Attaining Buddhahood in This Lifetime

With acknowledgement to Nichiren, a thirteenth century Japanese Buddhist monk who established his own 'school' based on the *Lotus Sutra*, devotion to the sutra entails the chanting of *Namu Myōhō Renge Kyō* "homage to the *Lotus Sutra*". The following is a letter he wrote in which I have substituted this chanting with recognizing, and identifying, with Pure Awareness; and also substituted referring to the Lotus Sutra with investigation of our moment to moment experience which reveals the Pure Awareness, the constant conscious subjective presence, that underlies the whole of reality. The only rider I would like to add is that, although I believe that becoming aware of, and identifying, with Pure Awareness is the most direct path to awakening, I do **not** believe that it is the only one.

.

If you wish to free yourself from the sufferings of birth and death you have endured since time without beginning and to attain without fail unsurpassed enlightenment in this lifetime, you must perceive the mystic truth that is originally inherent in all living beings. Which is that you, and all things, are Consciousness – which is 'Pure Awareness' when at rest, and manifestation when in motion. Realizing that you essentially are 'Pure Awareness' will therefore enable you to grasp the mystic truth innate in all life, which is Consciousness itself.

This reality is the Mystic Law. It is called the Mystic Law because it reveals the principle of the mutually inclusive relationship of a single moment of life and all phenomena. That is why this sutra is the wisdom of all Buddhas. Life (Consciousness) at each moment encompasses the body and mind and the self and environment of all sentient beings in the Ten Worlds as well as all insentient beings in the three thousand realms, including plants, sky, earth, and even the minutest particles of dust. Life at each moment permeates the entire realm of phenomena and is revealed in all phenomena. To be awakened to this principle is itself the mutually inclusive relationship of life at each moment and all phenomena.

Nevertheless, even though you believe that you are 'Pure Awareness', if you think the Law is outside yourself, you are embracing not the Mystic Law but an inferior teaching. Which means those other than this realization, which are all expedient and provisional. No expedient or provisional teaching leads directly to enlightenment, and without the direct path to enlightenment you cannot attain Buddhahood, even if you practice lifetime after lifetime for countless kalpas. Attaining Buddhahood in this lifetime is then impossible. Therefore you must summon up deep faith that you are Pure Awareness and confirm this by deeply investigating this moment to moment experience. You must never think that any of the eighty thousand sacred teachings of Shakyamuni Buddha's lifetime or any of the Buddhas and bodhisattvas of the ten directions and three existences are outside yourself.

Your practice of the Buddhist teachings will not relieve you of the sufferings of birth and death in the least unless you perceive the true nature of your life, that you are Pure Awareness. If you seek enlightenment outside yourself, then your performing even ten thousand practices and ten thousand good deeds will be in vain. It is like the case of a poor man who spends night and day counting his neighbour's wealth but gains not even half a coin. That is why the T'ien-t'ai school's commentary states, "Unless one perceives the nature of one's life, one cannot eradicate one's grave offences." This passage implies that, unless one perceives the nature of one's life, one's practice will become an endless, painful austerity. Therefore, such students of Buddhism are condemned as non-Buddhist. Great Concentration and Insight states that, although they study Buddhism, their views are no different from those of non-Buddhists.

Whether you chant the Buddha's name, recite the sutra, or merely offer flowers and incense, all your virtuous acts will implant benefits and roots of goodness in your life. But true enlightenment is to discover your Buddha Nature, Pure Awareness. With this conviction you should strive in faith. The Vimalakirti Sutra states that, when one seeks the Buddhas' emancipation in the minds of ordinary beings, one finds that ordinary beings are the entities of enlightenment, and that the sufferings of birth and death are nirvana. It also states that, if the minds of living beings are impure, their land is also impure, but if their minds are pure, so is their land. There are not two lands, pure or impure in themselves. The difference lies solely in the good or evil of our minds.

It is the same with a Buddha and an ordinary being. When deluded, one is called an ordinary being, but when enlightened, one is called a Buddha. This is similar to a tarnished mirror that will shine like a jewel when polished. A mind now clouded by the illusions of the innate darkness of life is like a tarnished mirror, but when polished, it is sure to become like a clear mirror, reflecting the essential nature of phenomena and the true aspect of reality. Arouse deep faith, and diligently polish your mirror day and night. How should you polish it? By realizing that you are 'Pure Awareness' and not a separate self.

What then does *the mystic law* signify? It is simply the mysterious
nature of our life from moment to moment, which the mind cannot
comprehend or words express. When we look into our own mind at
any moment, we perceive neither colour nor form to verify that it
exists. Yet we still cannot say it does not exist, for many differing
thoughts continually occur. The mind cannot be considered either to
exist or not to exist. Life is indeed an elusive reality that transcends
both the words and concepts of existence and non-existence. It is
neither existence nor non-existence, yet exhibits the qualities of
both. It is the Pure Awareness in which perceptions and the mind
appear.

If we understand that our life at this moment is *this flow of objects
appearing in This,* then we will also understand that our life at other
moments is the Mystic Law. This realization is the mystic sutra, the
direct path to enlightenment, for it explains that the entity of our life,
which manifests either good or evil at each moment, is in fact the
entity of the Mystic Law. If you become aware of, and identify with,
Awareness with deep faith in this principle, you are certain to attain
Buddhahood in this lifetime. Never doubt in the slightest. But
notice that any doubts are just thoughts appearing in Awareness.
Maintain your faith by investigation and attain Buddhahood in this
lifetime.

Twelve – The Radiance of Awareness

Elucidates the 'radiance of Awareness', explaining how this manifests and can be 'seen'.

I have often described the Self, the constant conscious subjective presence, our innermost fundamental vital essence, as 'Pure Pristine Radiant Awareness'. For me this is verified by self-inquiry for when I ask the question "Who am I?" it reveals 'radiant aware nothingness'; that is to say there are only the question, the awareness of the question and the nothingness relative to which the question is perceived. For all perceptions only occur relative to nothingness, sounds relative to silence, forms relative to space, thoughts relative to no-thought etc., and Awareness itself is the perceiver, whilst the radiance of Awareness gives the 'light' by which the perception may take place. Awareness is like a 'back-lit' screen (which provides the illumination) on which the mind 'sees' thoughts (including mental-images), sensations, feelings etc. and chooses those which it wishes to focus upon and 'process'. Or, to put it another way, it is like a limitless luminous languid lake, of Consciousness, in which the luminosity provides the facility for the ephemeral 'ripples' (the manifestations) to be aware of each other. This Awareness is also 'pure and pristine' for objects come and go in It, leaving It totally unchanged.

Here is an email exchange on this subject:

> Hello Colin
> I've just read your book Awareness of Awareness
> What do you mean by
> "notice every thought etc is 'seen' by the 'light' of Awareness i.e.

Awareness is radiant" ?

What is this?

XXXX

Dear XXXX, This description is a simile, in that I am not talking about physical light but about the 'illumination' by which anything is revealed. In physical terms for one to see anything there must be light shining upon it for it's reflection to be registered by the eyes. In terms of being aware of anything, thoughts, sensations or mental images, they must be 'illuminated' (able to be detected) for them to be apparent. And it is this 'illumination', which is a property of Awareness, that allows them to be 'seen' ... thus Awareness can be described as 'radiant' in that it has this 'illuminating' quality.

John Wren-Lewis described this as a 'deep but dazzling darkness' in that Awareness is Consciousness at rest and thus 'darkness' and yet it has this 'dazzling' quality by which things may be seen, or to put it another way, by which It can see the 'things' (motions occurring within It) that arise, abide and subside in It. I hope this makes it clearer, Love, Colin

Aware Nothingness/Dazzling Darkness

Hail Pure Awareness,

Consciousness at rest,

In This Aware Nothingness,

All appears to manifest.

Radiant Awareness,

Consciousness at rest,

By This Dazzling Darkness,

All is seen which manifests.

Serene Pristine Awareness,

From which all things are 'lent',

Into This Aware Nothingness

All return when totally 'spent'.

Thank you. I really appreciate your wisdom.

Yes, I know 'deep darkness' that is so comfortable and safe.

XXXX

I must add that this 'wisdom' is not mine but belongs to the Self and is readily available to all of its expressions and instruments (us!) if the illusory small self (body/mind/self-image) is negated. Here are two poems on these subjects:

Who am I?

When we ask 'who am I?'

We discover by and by,

Absolutely nothing there,

Radiant, pristine, ever aware.

From birth to death our life is a series

Of moment to moment experiences.

Comprising thoughts, sensations and mental images

And That which sees these in all of their stages.

A torrent of objects that come and go

In Awareness, the subject, by which we 'know'.

The constant conscious perceiving presence,

Neath body and mind, our ultimate essence.

The universal consciousness is Awareness whilst at rest,

Within which, in motion, the cosmos is manifest.

So in Awareness all things come and go,

As in stillness all movements ebb and flow.

Awareness is ever silent and still

Witnessing all vibrations that mill…

Thus It is omniscient and omnipresent,

The substratum from which all things are 'lent'.

In which they are perceived and reside,

Omnipotent for into This they subside.

Pure and pristine, by things unaffected,

By whose radiance they are detected.

Self-Referencing the Original Sin

When we say 'I'

If this denotes a separate being,

Then this is a lie,

Caused by not our true Self seeing.

For many this word signifies,

A personal individual object,

Herein the confusion lies,

Missing the constant conscious subject.

That in which mind and body come and go,

Awareness, consciousness at rest,

In which thoughts, images and sensations flow,

The essential level, the deepest.

If as an object we reference our-self,

Then this is the 'original sin'.

Overlooking Awareness, the Absolute Self,

Causing myriad problems to begin.

Self-grasping, aggrandizement, self-cherishing,

Self-promotion, continually thinking of the small self,

This endless list within which wisdom is perishing,

Contemplating power, possessions, position and pelf.

Whereas, if by 'I' we mean Awareness pure,

Of ourselves the fundamental essence,

Then this entails no problems that is sure,

Identified as the subjective presence.

In fact we need to avoid,

Any thought which objectifies the 'I',

Which is This and thus devoid,

Of characteristics … the subjective 'eye'.

Thirteen – 'Lord Of The Dance' and 'Simple Gifts'

A commentary on two well known spiritual 'folk' songs which share a common tune.

Lord Of The Dance

I danced in the morning when the world was young

The dance of Consciousness is the world ...

I danced in the moon and the stars and the sun

*It dances **as** the moon, the stars and the sun ...*

I came down from heaven and I danced on the earth

It is omnipresent and contains heaven and earth.

At Bethlehem I had my birth

A fully awakened expression of This, Jesus, appeared at Bethlehem.

Dance, dance, wherever you may be

We, as expressions of This, are enjoined to enjoy life ...

I am the lord of the dance, said he

*He, This Consciousness, **is** the dancer.*

And I lead you all, wherever you may be

In essence we are all This and thus led by This ...

And I lead you all in the dance, said he.

We are all That participating in the dance of life ...

Simple Gifts

'Tis the gift to be simple, 'tis the gift to be free

Realizing, we are Awareness, simplifies life and sets us free.

'Tis the gift to come down where we ought to be,

For we are no longer bound by the illusion of a separate self.

And when we find ourselves in the place just right,

Each moment is enough and thus everywhere is just right ...

'Twill be in the valley of love and delight.

We discover the bliss of being, from the peace at our centre.

When true simplicity is gained,

By realizing, that you are expressions of Awareness, and then ...

To bow and to bend we shan't be ashamed,

We will not be bound by self-image, and the ego.

To turn, turn will be our delight,

To flow with life will be natural and delightful,

Till by turning, turning we come 'round right'.

And by this flowing everywhere will be 'right'.

Fourteen – Nonduality and Native Americans

Discusses nonduality and Native American Spirituality based on the writings of Ohiyesa of the native Dakota, Sioux Nation.

Nonduality means 'not two' indicating that 'all is One' ... with no possibility of two or more. For me this means that it must include everything (and no thing!), leaving nothing excluded, denigrated or sidelined. I was musing over this whilst reading my friend (initial publisher, collaborator and manager/owner of www.nonduality.com) Jerry Katz' fine book *One – Essential Writings on Nonduality* and it came to me that the most inclusive view was given in the chapter *Native American Tradition – The Ways of The Spirit.*

Whereas many of the views given espouse certain elements, most commonly that of the Absolute, Brahman, Ein Sof, The Void, Allah, The Tao etc ... the Absolute Principle behind (and the source, container and dissolution of) the manifest universe, the chapter that really appealed to me was that based on Ohiyesa of the native Dakota, Sioux Nation. For this is a true honouring of all aspects of Reality, the manifest and unmanifest being of equal importance and thus this includes all aspects of life and not just the overtly 'spiritual' activities such as meditation, contemplation, prayer etc. As we shall see with this approach the whole of life becomes a spiritual activity for all is seen as a manifestation of the Great Spirit from which there is never, and can never be, any separation.

In this chapter many aspects of this (One!) are delineated and I shall consider them each in turn:

The Great Mystery

'The Eternal, the Great Mystery that surrounds us and embraces us, is the supreme conception, bringing with it the fullest measure of joy and satisfaction possible in this life.'[16]

This is Consciousness: that is Pure Awareness when at rest, and Cosmic Energy when in movement – the manifestation. The former is our essential being and the latter constitutes our physical being (body/mind), and as such This surrounds, embraces, and **is** us. The realization of This, and that we are not separate objects in a universe of such, brings about the greatest joy and satisfaction possible. For this reveals the innate joy, at the centre of our being, and we achieve satisfaction by seeing that we are instruments of This and thus everything we do is **as** This and is seen, known and enjoyed by This.

'The worship of the Great Mystery is silent, solitary, free from all self-seeking.'[17]

To realize This by becoming 'aware of (and identifying with) Awareness' requires no words just a direct seeing of the undeniable[18] existence of the Awareness in which thoughts, sensations and mental images are seen; and by which they are seen. This is necessarily a

---

[16] Katz, J. *One – Essential Writings on Nonduality*, 2007, Boulder, p.81
[17] Ibid
[18] For without there would be no awareness of our experience.

solitary activity, although the 'pointings' of others may facilitate it, which will entail negation of the (small) self and as such is free from all self-seeking, although it will also entail Self-finding! The Self being a synonym for the Great Mystery of which we are all expressions and instruments.

The Temple of Nature

'The One who may be met in the mysterious, shadowy aisles of the primeval forest or on the sunlit bosom of virgin prairies, upon dizzy spires and pinnacles of naked rock, and in the vast jewelled vault of the night sky ... such a God needs no lesser cathedral.'[19]

For as the One (Consciousness) constitutes the whole of manifestation then It may be (and is) met everywhere, requiring no special location for such a meeting to take place. In fact if viewed from this standpoint then everything can directly reveal Reality, for our experience of anything is a combination of thought (including mental-images) and sensation and all of these appear in and are seen by Awareness, the former being Consciousness in motion and the latter That at rest, which is the Reality. For more on this see 'Every Thought and Sensation Reveal Reality' in *Beyond The Separate Self.* Also, when nature is seen from Pure Awareness, with a still mind - unencumbered by the filter of small 'self' and its many contractions, then it appears much more

---

[19] Katz, J. *One – Essential Writings on Nonduality*, 2007, Boulder, p.82

beautiful, vivid and alive than when seen through misidentification as the small self (body/mind).

The Power of Silence

'We profoundly believe in silence ... holy silence is God's voice ... it is the Great Mystery. its fruits are self-control, true courage, patience, dignity and reverence.'[20]

Consciousness, is totally silent when at rest, as Pure Awareness, for by definition noise is vibration and thus in movement. This is the Eternal, unchanging aspect of the Divine; whereas the aspect of Cosmic Energy, Consciousness in movement, is ephemeral and always changing. So, if we define God as Eternal and unchanging, then silence is indeed his 'voice' (or lack of it!). When identified with, and as, Consciousness then the mind's interminable chatter (which is fuelled by misidentification as a separate object in a world of such) abates leaving long periods of silence. Even during misidentification there are such moments between the thoughts and it is these moments that are especially auspicious for becoming 'aware of Awareness' (the Great Mystery) for this requires direct seeing, which is hampered by focussing on thoughts instead of the silence between them. This Awareness itself is always silent, purely reflecting what appears in It and the mind notices those reflections that it considers important and

---

[20] Ibid

wishes to 'process'. It is when the mind is in abeyance, not processing, that nature (every thing) is seen 'as it is' and in its true glory as an expression of Consciousness Itself. When correctly identified with Awareness then (small) self-negation, fearlessness, patience, dignity and reverence are natural by-products, and outcomes, of this awakening.

The Power of Spirit

'The whole created universe shares in the immortal perfection of its Maker. The spirit pervades all creation ... the tree, the waterfall, the grizzly bear, each is an embodied Force and as such an object of reverence.'[21]

All is of the same essence, Consciousness Itself, and thus shares the same immortal perfection and is an object of reverence. For this to be seen one needs to be awake, identified with (and as) this Consciousness. The reason I stress the aspect of Awareness (the spirit) – This at rest – is that this is unchanging, whereas Cosmic Energy – the manifest, This in motion – is ever changing and arises in, exists in and returns to Awareness. For all movement arises in (and from) stillness, exists in a substratum of stillness, and finally returns to stillness. Thus at the deepest level Awareness is the essence of all ...

---

[21] Ibid p.82-83

Poverty and Simplicity

'Virtue and happiness are independent of material things. It is the rule of our life to share with our less fortunate brothers and sisters. Thus we keep our spirits free from pride, avarice and envy.'[22]

Virtue and happiness are the natural outcomes of awakening and thus independent of any 'thing', as awakening entails realizing that we are not a 'thing' but our body/minds are ephemeral expressions, and instruments, of Awareness Itself. Thus we also realize that all 'others' are essentially the same and sharing becomes natural, in fact the first 'stage' of the Bodhisattva path entails cultivating the 'perfection' of giving. In this pride, avarice and envy become things of the past, as they all rely on misidentification of ourselves and 'others' as separate individual objects.

The Importance of Prayer

'Prayer – the daily recognition of the Unseen and the Eternal – is our one inevitable duty. We recognise the spirit in all creation, whenever we come upon a scene that is strikingly beautiful we pause for an instant in the attitude of worship'.[23]

---

[22] Ibid p.83
[23] Ibid p.84

115

Daily recognition is vitally important for we have so long misidentified ourselves as an object that we need to nurture our awakening to the realization that we are Pure Awareness. In fact I recommend that one spends three periods of twenty minutes (or more) relaxing into 'awareness of Awareness', and thus correct identification, every day. This will slowly forge new neural pathways in the brain and living through these will become more natural than employing the old paradigm of misidentification. This is recognition of the Unseen and Eternal, for Awareness is both of these. The recognition of all manifestation as an expression of This is to 'recognise the spirit in all creation' and strikingly beautiful scenes have the power to make this apparent by 'stopping the mind'. This reveals That (silent Awareness) which is deeper than mind and also allows us to appreciate the scene 'as it is' and not through the erroneous filter of misidentification … which creates an attitude of worship, or of wonder.

The Appreciation of Beauty

'We hold nature to be the measure of consummate beauty and we consider its destruction to be a sacrilege. Beauty, in our eyes, is always fresh and living, even as God, the Great Mystery, dresses the world anew at each season of the year.'[24]

---

[24] Ibid p.86-87

This follows directly from seeing everything 'as it is' an expression of the One, Consciousness, God, the Great Mystery, call it what you will. The natural world is nearly always more varied, and beautiful, than any art created by man; for this latter tends to be influenced by, and created through, the particular filters of the mind in question. When there is identification as Awareness then reverence for nature is spontaneous and its destruction will always be avoided where possible. This natural beauty is always fresh and living, not only in form but also in essence - which is Consciousness Itself, the life-force of all.

The Miracle of the Ordinary

'We see miracles on every hand – the miracle of life in the seed and egg, the miracle of death in a lightning flash and in the swelling deep. We all have to face the ultimate miracle – the origin and principle of life. In the presence of this mystery the Indian beholds with awe the Divine in all creation'.[25]

Regarding this I wrote in 'The Miraculous and The Auspicious' (in *Awareness of Awareness – The Open* Way):

> With regard to miracles, once the filter of the small self is
> removed then the world is seen to be miraculous moment by
> moment. Also, when examined, the myriad expressions (and

---

[25]Ibid p.87

evolutions) of Consciousness are seen to be miracles. So in this paradigm every moment is auspicious and every 'thing' is miraculous, meaning that one need not wait for an auspicious day to begin the journey of self-discovery and one need not hang on to anything as being of more significance than anything else. For everything is significant and full of meaning being varying expressions of the one Absolute Consciousness.

For the Ultimate Miracle is indeed Consciousness – the origin and principle of life, and to realize this is to behold in awe the Divine in all creation.

Summing up, the Native American attitude does indeed encompass everything within, and as, an expression of the One Great Mystery, leaving nothing excluded ... which is true Nonduality.

Fifteen – Om Namah Sivaya

This chapter gives multiple uses for the mantra 'Om Namah Sivaya' –
Hail Pure Awareness, The Totality of Being.

The mantra 'Om Namah Sivaya' can be used in three ways to take one beyond the separate self:

1/ Kirtan: The singing of God's name, in this case this mantra, in which one 'loses oneself' in devotion and the enthusiasm of the chant. One of the easiest ways to go beyond the separate self if one just lets go of all inhibition and sings with one's whole being, for no-one else is judging you (or anyone else) as all are participating with the same aim ...

2/ Meditation: When repeated mentally the mantra sets up an internal 'vibrational field' which, it is posited, is very beneficial both physically and spiritually. If repeated with enough mental concentration this can also still the mind which can reveal the '*nothingness*' behind all manifestation. However this requires a supreme effort of will which can take many years to achieve.

3: Contemplation/ Direct Seeing, which itself has three components:

a: The meaning of the mantra:

'Om' represents the Totality of all that is – the manifest and the unmanifest – Consciousness at rest and in movement.

'Namah' means 'salutations' (to) or 'in praise' (of).

'Sivaya', (of) Siva, which is the 'total Godhead', the 'Supreme Reality'. Siva represents Universal Consciousness - when it is at rest, aware of every movement occurring in it, this is **Pure Awareness**. When in movement this is cosmic energy – the dance of Siva – of which all manifestation is constituted, for matter and energy are synonymous.

So one reading of the mantra is: 'In praise of Siva the Totality of All that is.'

> Pure Awareness,
> Consciousness at rest,
> Within Which nothing less,
> Than all appears to manifest.

> Radiant Awareness,
> Consciousness at rest,
> By Which nothing less,
> Than all is seen which manifests.

> Pristine Awareness,
> Consciousness at rest,
> Into Which the manifest,
> Returns to nothingness.

b: The '*awareness*' of the mantra repetition:

As one repeats the mantra there is effortless, and choiceless, *awareness* of this repetition. This very *awareness* is, in itself, that which the mantra is addressing. By recognition of this one can see that the mantra directly points to that which it is extolling, *Pure Awareness*. If one remains mindful of this, whilst repeating the mantra, then the 'revelation' has taken place. Alternatively repetition of the mantra immediately reminds one of this *Pure Awareness*, our true 'spiritual inheritance'.

c: The '*nothingness*' in which the mantra arises, exists, is 'known', and subsides:

This is the '*nothingness*' which can be revealed by repeating the mantra with intense concentration, thus blocking out all other 'things' from the mind. However this *nothingness* may be immediately realized by seeing that every 'thing' appears in *nothingness*, exists in *nothingness*, is known by contrast to *nothingness*, and disappears back into *nothingness*. Without this background of *nothingness*, as a contrast, there would not be *awareness* of any 'thing'.

Once one has truly become aware of this 'Aware Nothingness' one has entered into what the Native Americans call "The Great Mystery' for This is The Absolute Reality - Brahman, Allah, Yahweh, The Void, Rigpa, Big Mind, The Tao, The Great Spirit – call it what you will.

Sixteen – The Tricky Mind

This talks about the 'tricky mind' and gives three examples of how it tries to remain in control by trivializing, or overlooking, 'awakening'.

I never cease to be amazed at the trickiness of the mind and its ability to send its owner off on wild goose chases when it is threatened by the search for, or discovery of, freedom. This is not surprising for until the search is ultimately successful the mind has been in control as the supreme power, actually who one thinks one is, and it will not give this up lightly even when it becomes startlingly obvious that this is not the case. Several examples from my recent interactions with people, who have had 'moments of sweet delight, of pure simple recognition, the alchemy of presence, when someone sees themselves as they truly are' (Gangaji) and who have themselves deeply investigated the nature of Reality, will demonstrate this.

A good friend complained that her mind would give her no rest and that she had just been on a meditation retreat, which had helped, and was going to go on many more. Whilst meditation has its place, unless it leads to insight it tends to be used as a method to still the mind which may have some temporary effect, but this soon wears off when the session is over. This stilling of the mind requires much practice over long periods to be successful and although it provides fleeting peace, whilst the meditation is taking place, it does not lead to freedom as the mind remains in control (a classic trick) even whilst stifling its own meanderings! Not only that, but in many cases the attempt is unsuccessful as the mind reacts by going into overdrive and becoming even more restless as it 'bucks' under the attempt to stifle it by concentration. This leads to feelings of frustration, and failure, rather than the expected results of peace and happiness. Also meditation can subtly stop you being in the present moment by positing that you will attain something in the future if you 'sit' diligently... Thus, as you sit, whatever may have been the direction from your Meditation Master, there is naturally some anticipation of a future result. Whereas freedom is always here and now, requiring direct seeing which in turn leads to a still mind, rather than stilling the mind in attempt to become free...

For more on this see 'The Case Against Sitting Meditation' in *Awakening and Beyond*; rather than meditation I recommend relaxing into 'awareness of Awareness' in which case the restless mind is no problem as I elucidated in 'Restless Mind ... No Problem!' in *A Light Unto Your Self*. That is not to say that I do not also meditate but only as a way of strengthening my 'seeing' of the Aware Nothingness that has already been discovered, for more on this see 'Mantra as a Vehicle of Revelation' in *Beyond The Separate Self*. This is a case in which meditation is used as a method to deepen one's pre-existing insight rather than a technique to still the mind.

Another friend was talking about attachment which he regards as a major obstacle in achieving freedom and was postulating that for many women their attachment to, and love of, their children and family is detrimental in their search for liberation. I actually totally disagree with this, see 'Non-attachment and Love' in *The Happiness That Needs Nothing*, but do agree that there is one attachment which totally bars one's access to freedom and that is the attachment to the small self, that is regarding oneself as an individual separate entity (or object) in a universe of such. For most people this entails identifying with their illusory mind created self-image, which is another devious ploy by the mind to stay in control. In fact at a deeper level this entails identifying with the mind itself and when you look at nearly all western therapies designed to overcome mental health problems this is an implicit assumption, that the patient is his (or her) mind (in a body) and if we can only sort that out then everything will be alright! Which can never ultimately succeed, but only act as a bandaid, for identification with the mind, and as a separate object, is the underlying cause of most (needless) mental suffering and existential angst. In fact it seems to me that the idea that one should overcome all attachment ('affection or fondness' OED) in order to become awakened is another trick of the mind to prevent this. For it sets an impossible task which will either deter one from seeking freedom, or will be like the huge rock that Sisyphus was doomed to eternally roll up the steep hill only for it to fall back to the bottom again! Whereas overcoming attachment to the (illusory) small self is eminently possible once one has discovered the true Self and if one honours (by staying true to) this discovery. In fact once awakening has taken place this can lead to falling in love with the whole of existence (except the illusory small self!) in other words the ultimate attachment! In this case there is no clinging, for as things come and go (which they will) there is left no lack (or hole) by their departure, as one is still engulfed in (and by) the beloved. Actually 'clinging' is a more accurate word for what causes pain and misidentification, rather than 'attachment', and it is this clinging to the small self which must be negated. To return to my friend's comment, it is natural to have deep love (attachment) for one's family and children, but it is this clinging to these (and anyone or thing) that is the result of misidentification and causes needless suffering.

Finally, another friend, who is an anti-capitalism activist, said to me that we were both working to 'awaken' people but that her method is more effective as it engages more people, whereas mine is more cerebral and intellectual appealing to a smaller percentage of the population. She writes articles, produces pamphlets and addresses meetings about the dangers of globalisation, big business and capitalism in general. Now this activity may indeed 'awaken' people to these dangers, but it is hardly designed to relieve their angst or actually help them in any way, for taking up this cause is also like rolling the Sisyphean rock … an activity which uses a great deal of effort and is liable to get nowhere. Relating to this see my article 'Awareness and The Environment' in *Awakening and Beyond* in which I argue that the best way to overcome greed (for goods, power, money etc...) is to awaken to the truth of who (or what) one actually **is**, and to encourage as many as one can to do likewise, for in this awakening greed is naturally negated as one discovers the innate happiness and joy at the core of our being … requiring nothing! Needless to say this also negates all existential angst and unnecessary mental suffering which anti establishment activism only exacerbates. That is not to say that I am against activism but awakening to one's essential being, and helping others to do this, should be the framework within which this activity should take place. For, without this, the desire for such activity is just another trick of the mind to keep one busy and avoid 'upsetting the applecart' by discovering (or honouring if the discovery has already been made) that one's essential identity is much 'greater' than it, thus relegating it to it's rightful place as an instrument ... the servant not the master.

Seventeen – Honouring The Obvious

An antidote to the 'tricky mind' by honoring what has been discovered and seeing all of its tricks as ephemeral thoughts appearing in Awareness.

When I wrote my first book *Beyond The Separate Self* I believed that what it was saying was so self-evident that I was tempted to call it *The Bleeding Obvious*! I decided against this as it seemed to me that there might be some consumer resistance to such a title as, if what it was saying was indeed 'bleeding obvious', why should anybody (appear stupid enough to) need to buy it … and even, if they did, they would keep it hidden so as not to appear stupid! However, I still am of the opinion that its contents, or at least the main thrust of them, are obvious and it is this that prevents them from being valued after they have been seen. In fact the absolute simplicity of awakening that they espouse goes 'against the grain' of what the many religions and spiritual paths say and this simplicity allows the mind to negate them by saying "well if it's that simple why aren't we all awakened?" Even if they are fully seen the mind still tends to search for more ecstatic and esoteric experiences available from paths that have more complications and practices. For this searching for more and more is a classic trick of the mind to keep us enchained … see the previous article 'The Tricky Mind'.

So what is so bleeding obvious and shall I state it ?! Just the fact that, for each of us, at this moment (and all moments) there are thoughts, mental images, feelings and sensations; and it is the awareness of these that constitutes our direct experience. This has been the case since our birth and, even when asleep, awareness is present (although in abeyance) ready for dreams that may occur or physical sensations that may become strong enough to wake us up. Within this the thoughts, mental images, feelings and sensations are ever changing objects (the perceived) whist the awareness is a constant subjective presence (the perceiver). As I am sure that we all think that we have been present since our birth, then we are this latter, the subjective presence - awareness, rather than the flow of thoughts, mental images, feelings and sensations. It is this flow of objects which constitute (our experience of) our body/minds behind which, or deeper than, there exists this constant conscious subjective presence that **we essentially are**. For if we identify with, or as, the body/mind we are identifying with an ever changing torrent of ephemeral objects rather than that which has witnessed our entire lives.

Identifying with, and as, awareness itself has profound consequences which I have espoused in many articles, most notably 'Identifying With Awareness Creates a World View' in *Freedom From Anxiety and Needless Suffering* and 'Self Identity – The Key To Spontaneous Living' in *The Happiness That Needs Nothing'*. However, for many who have truly seen that they are awareness the mind negates this 'seeing' by trivialising it (another classic trick) so that it may resume control. So this is where we need to commit to, and honour, this 'seeing' by valuing it highly and negate the mind's trivialisation of it by seeing that this activity is just another series of thoughts coming and going in awareness (what we actually are!) - for we are aware of them. Note during this (and forever as it happens …) we **are not the mind** which is actually just an instrument for our use. It has to be forcibly put back into its place when it attempts to take over by us using it as an instrument against itself, or I should say against its ingrained assumption that it is who we are ... it is not! Also all doubts are to be treated in the same manner as ephemeral thoughts coming and going in awareness which, when examined, they undoubtedly are. Do not allow it to resume control by being lazy, or allowing it to objectify you with any of the many labels that you have applied (it has applied) to yourself before you awakened. None of them has the slightest validity for **you are not an object**! Every time you are tempted to re-objectify yourself just see that this temptation and all of its consequences are just fleeting thought patterns that have become ingrained, this seeing will negate them and lessen their hold over you. In fact they have no hold over whom you actually are, awareness itself, but the mind will try to use them to regain control ... **don't let it**!

The actual seeing that one is awareness is so simple that it only requires to be honoured by holding true to it to overcome all needless mental suffering and existential angst. So if any of these come up this is a sign that misidentification is occurring and they should be used (immediately!) to reinvestigate and discover that **one is awareness**. This can be done in the simple way just given or for a more thorough investigation, which also reveals the 'properties' of awareness itself (which you are!) see the appendix. The more often one discovers that one is awareness the less misidentification will occur, for this repeated discovery will forge new neural pathways in the brain and as this happens those associated with misidentification will gradually fall into disuse. Above all be vigilant to the mind's many tricks to resume control which are easily spotted by the discomfort, or contractions, that they cause and can thus be used as a signal to resume the investigation. After a while the mind will become accustomed to its new (proper) role and will stop causing mischief … it will become a wonderful servant rather than a terrible master!

When this occurs it naturally quietens down as all of the self-analysis, self-serving, self-aggrandizement, self-loathing, self-preserving, self-interest etc… ceases for one has truly discovered that there is no separate self! Then life becomes much easier as it (the mind) solves problems naturally and spontaneously, for it is fulfilling its actual function as a facilitatory device for enabling us to live in the world. For the mind/body is actually an expression, and instrument, of Consciousness (awareness when at rest and matter/energy when in motion) through which That can engage with, know and love Its own manifestation.

Eighteen – Discussion on Vipassana Meditation

An email discussion about (Vipassana) meditation resulting from a response to my article 'The Tricky Mind'.

Here is an email exchange in response to my article, 'The Trickery of The Mind' regarding the section on meditation, note that his emails are in italics.

Hi Colin

Meditation "practice", or at least the Vipassana kind that I have had some experience with, seems to me quite valuable. Some time ago I realised that Vipassana is not all that different to the practice recommended by Ramana Maharshi: "Ask who and I, and rest in what happens." Or Nisargadatta Maharaja, who recommended to "Stay with the 'I am' and it will reveal its secrets."

Some years ago I spent some time in a meditation monastery in Burma where we did intensive sitting and walking whilst staying with the sense of presence. After a few months, I came to a sense of peace and tranquillity I had never experienced before (nor since). Yes, it did wear off, in time. Nevertheless, I believe I got a taste of the great beyond through that simple practice of just watching whatever arises: sounds, smells, thoughts, emotions, body aches and pains etc

My own impression today is that so long as you do not expect anything from meditation practice it is very valuable. This is a great paradox: if you somehow are sitting and walking in order to achieve something, then of course nothing much will happen. But if you can let go, and of course you cant do anything anyway, something interesting may indeed happen. Just as in sleep one gets a taste of the divine, it can happen also, as Buddha discovered, just by watching the breath arise and pass away. ...

Dear XXXX, I do agree that meditation has its place as I wrote: 'Whilst meditation has its place, unless it leads to insight it tends to be used as a method to still the mind which may have some temporary effect, but this soon wears off when the session is over.' So it is valuable if it stills the mind, even more valuable if it leads to insight and would be most valuable if it led to liberation, complete freedom from existential angst and misidentification. Unfortunately, as John Wren Lewis said, "meditation might be a way but the results don't seem to be very promising. I have spoken to many people who have meditated for years and none of them can describe coming from a state like this (awakening) ... I have only met four people who can and none of them did it through meditation". I also have never met anyone who was awakened through meditation[26], they may have achieved many trance states, a still mind and even psychic powers but still suffered from existential angst and the feeling that there was more to achieve. In fact I meditated twice daily for between 45-60 minutes at each session for

---

[26] That is not to say that there are not such people, just that I have never met one. I am sure that, for some, meditation has led to complete awakening when combined with insight and intuition.

over 15 years and the previous statement applies exactly to my experience. It was only when I met Gangaji who said "Be still. Stop. Give up all effort and see what is there when you ask 'who am I?'" that I had my first real glimpse of the Ultimate Reality.

I know that you have said that Vipassana is very similar to this but that was not my experience when I went to my first, and last, Vipassana retreat. It was seven years ago, 12 years after my 'awakening' whilst I was nearing completion of 'Beyond The Separate Self', and I went in the hope of just being able to sit immersed deeply into my own 'being'. However, this was not possible as we were virtually forced to practice the specific technique, by repeated reminders through speakers at regular intervals. This technique I described at the time as feeling to me like 'swimming through mud' and I could see no value in it[27] for it appeared to be like scrabbling up a mountain that I could be on the top of in a single bound. In fact all it took was to re-realise that 'I am Pure Awareness' and there I was! When I told the nun in charge she said that I was not pure enough ... which from her point of view may well have been true, but direct seeing of one's own essential being (and living from that 'seeing') is more important, and valuable, than following any set of precepts! The other thing that I was very aware of was how dejected and downcast all the participants appeared to be, even those who were returning after many other retreats. When I decided to leave

---

[27] For a more comprehensive and complementary look at Vipassana see the next chapter. I am only reporting on my direct experience at the time.

the support staff, who were amazed at my joy, enthusiasm and good humour, kept asking me what I 'did' to enable this ...

I have since talked to many people who have been on Vipassana retreats and cannot find one who credits it for their awakening. I had a good friend in Sydney who went yearly for many years and was finally told not to attend as it seemed she was not getting the expected benefit of it. She would arrive home refreshed and invigorated with a much stiller mind, but within a few weeks was back to her old angst ridden self. I also have a good friend who is the head of a large foundation that promotes Vipassana style meditation, has written books on the subject, and is actually leading a weekend retreat for meditation teachers as I write this. Even he is now searching for more and has recently joined a bhakti sect in India which promotes awakening people with Shaktipat, awakening by laying on of hands by an enlightened being. They are currently in a month of intense sadhana where many 'miracles' have been reported...

That said, I am sure if one can just sit, with no expectation, immersed in Pure Awareness then this is very insightful and nourishing. In fact it is very similar to my own method of relaxing into 'awareness of Awareness' ... of which the attachment[28] is one form, Love, Colin

Here is his reply:

---

[28] See article 'Relaxing Into Awareness of Awareness'.

'Whilst meditation has its place, unless it leads to insight it tends to be used as a method to still the mind which may have some temporary effect, but this soon wears off when the session is over.' So it is valuable if it stills the mind, even more valuable if it leads to insight and would be most valuable if it led to liberation, complete freedom from existential angst and misidentification.

Yes, this is more or less my understanding as well.

I was very lucky when I first took up Vipassana that the teacher (Joseph Goldstein, about 1980) offered no ritual. All one was asked to do was sit and note whatever arose—thoughts, feelings, sounds, smells, emotions, body pains, judgements--and once noted, coming back to the breath as an anchor.

Later I went to Burma that winter to the Meditation monastery the abbot of which was Mahasi Sayadaw who had delved deeply into the original sutras said to have been handed down from Buddha. The abbot retranslated from the Pali language into Burmese and then English and this became the source of modern Vipassana we know in the west.* I was very lucky, looking back on it, that Mahasi Sayadaw was dying of cancer and did not give interviews. His assistants, who spoke almost no English, had only one thing to say when, at our weekly interview, we *westerners asked questions about the practice. All they could say was "Keep trying". To every question that was their answer! Only later did I realize how lucky I was when I went to other Vipassana retreats and had similar experiences to what you found. (By "keep trying" they meant trying to keep your attention on whatever was arising.) ("Breathing in, he knows breathing in, hearing a sound he knows hearing, smelling a smell he knows smelling, thought arising he knows thinking. . ." is what the sutras claim that Buddha said.)*

Dear XXXX, I noticed you said (in the first email) ' I came to a sense of peace and tranquillity I had never experienced before (nor since).' My question is 'who' is not at peace and what can disturb the tranquillity of Pure Awareness?

Yes, I had to use language to say that "peace and tranquillity arose". . .

And you might say that anything that arose and passed away cannot be the final truth: namely what is there always and beyond forever. Agreed. The shift at that level is not yet seen. Clouds are still blocking the sun, or appear to be.

Dear XXXX, The 'clouds' are mind created and illusory ... it reminds me of Papaji's famous comment that the final obstacle (to awakening) is the belief that there is an obstacle! What is required is for you to have faith in, and honour - stay true to, your own 'knowing'. For whilst you think there are clouds blocking the sun these thoughts are the clouds! See the attachment (Honouring the Obvious) which I wrote as the direct follow up to 'The Tricky Mind', Love, Colin

Dear XXXX, I have put our exchange together in an article which I am sending to you for your approval, or at least permission to use.

"Breathing in, he knows breathing in, hearing a sound he knows hearing, smelling a smell he knows smelling, thought arising he knows thinking. . ." This is awareness of what is occurring through (or to) the body/mind, a small step away from seeing that these breaths, sounds, smells, thoughts etc occur in Awareness itself, for he is aware of them. Which is then 'awareness of Awareness' for he is then noticing (aware of) Awareness itself, and just effortlessly resting in that 'seeing' is 'relaxing into awareness of Awareness', Love, Colin

Thank you. Feel free to disseminate if you wish.

Thanks ... It was a useful exchange for me to hear that there are teachers of Vipassana with a more 'free' take, promoting a less rigid method, Love, Colin

P.s. All the best with your upcoming retreat.

Nineteen – An Introduction to Vipassana Meditation

An introduction to Vipassana meditation, which is widely practiced, by considering a book on the subject by Joseph Goldstein – a famous teacher, referenced in the previous chapter as one with a more 'open' approach to Vipassana.

Following on from the previous chapter the name Joseph Goldstein rang a bell and I remembered an assignment I did, for my double degree in Philosophy and Religion, back in 2004 reviewing one of his books. I have included it here as it gives a useful introduction to Vipassana meditation, and Buddhism in general. Although I had a negative experience with this type of meditation his variety of it is much freer than the one I encountered, and I know that many people have benefited from it. Also the essay gives a useful introduction to many key Buddhist ideas and practices.

The purpose of this essay is to discuss the use of 'The Experience Of Insight' by Joseph Goldstein as a guide to meditation. In fact its secondary title is 'A Simple and Direct Guide to Meditation', and thus it is 'a priori' designed for such a purpose.

This book is a series of talks given over thirty days at a Vipassana meditation retreat and contains instructions on the technique of, and philosophy behind Vipassana meditation. The technique is from the Theravadan tradition which means that it stems from the early teachings of the Buddha.

"Theravada purports to follow the 'teaching' which is 'ancient' and 'primordial' (thera): that is, the Buddha's teaching. Whilst it has not remained static it has kept close to the early teachings of Buddhism, and preserved their emphasis on attaining liberation by 'ones' own efforts using the Dhamma as a guide' (An introduction to Buddhism' P. Harvey page 2)

This is in contrast to the 'Mahayana which is characterized, on the one hand, by devotion to a number of holy saviour beings, and on the other by several sophisticated philosophies developed by extending the implications of earlier teachings.' (Ibid page 2)

The word Vipassana means insight, or wisdom, and thus the purpose of meditation is to develop insight into the nature of reality. Thus a thirty day retreat of rigorous Vipassana meditation fully satisfies Harvey's definition of "emphasis on attaining liberation by 'ones' own efforts".

A word or two needs to be said with regard to Joseph Goldstein's spiritual lineage to appreciate the origin of this form of Vipassana meditation. Formally meditation was regarded as strictly for monks only, but around the turn of the twentieth century this began to be questioned in Burma. It was considered that time was getting short and that for the maximum number of people to achieve enlightenment there needed to be a drastic increase in the number of people meditating. Also the older 'Jhanic' meditations were beginning to be superseded by simpler Vipassana meditation:

> The classic Pali Canon structure of meditational progression is intended primarily for the monk who will follow the Jhanic progression towards Nibbana. Vipassana the understanding of

all experiences and states, including the jhanas, as impermanent...leads on to the crowning attainment of cessation. But since the Vipassana understanding is the quintessence of the insight leading to Nibbana...it is implied in the sacred scripture that Vipassana alone could be a discipline sufficient for salvation. (P116, 'Theravada Meditation' Winston L King)

This Vipassana meditation has now become central to popular Theravada Buddhism through a movement of 'lay meditation' which originated in Burma. One of the initiators of this was Ledi Sayadaw who 'in his concern for all Buddhists to work towards their final salvation whilst there was time and opportunity , he urged that any and all should at least begin meditation.' (Ibid P.120) Through his disciple U Ba Khin who was 'fully persuaded that Vipassana was the quintessence of the Buddha's teachings and that it could be practiced in connection with daily work' (Ibid P.125) and then through Goenka and Angarika Sri Munindra we reach Joseph Goldstein who is actively promoting Vipassana meditation through teaching, writing, instructing and holding retreats.

Moving on to the text itself it starts on day 1, naturally, with 'opening and beginning instructions'. This commences with explaining the practice of 'taking refuge', about which Paul Williams says (on page 21 of 'Buddhist Thought') "The minimum for becoming a Buddhist is spoken of as three times 'taking the triple refuge' in the way prescribed by Buddhist tradition." So this taking of refuge in the Buddha (and his qualities), the Dhamma (his teachings) and the Sangha (the Buddhist community) is central to 'being a Buddhist'.

Next Goldstein goes on to explain the five moral precepts: not killing, not stealing, not indulging in sexual misconduct, not lying and not taking of intoxicants. About this he says on page 2 of 'The Experience Of Insight' (hereafter denoted by TEOI) 'Following these precepts will provide a strong base for the development of concentration and will make the growth of insight possible.' Then after discussing patience, silence and keeping to oneself he goes on to describe the actual meditation practice itself. This is 'breath awareness' with attention either on the rising/falling of the abdomen or on the tip of the nose. Following this he discusses walking meditation with awareness of the lifting, moving and placing of the foot in each step. Finally he gives the daily schedule which includes eight hours of sitting and four to five hours of walking meditation!

Over the next twenty nine days he gives a series of talks which I have classified into three main groups: Buddha's Philosophy, Direct Meditation Instructions, and General Buddhist Thought/information and Stories:

1/ Buddha's Philosophy, in which he discusses:

The Noble Eightfold Path (on day 2) consisting of 'right: view, directed thought, speech, action, livelihood, effort, mindfulness, and concentration' (Harvey p68)

The three pillars of Dharma (on day 12) which are three fields of action which cultivate and strengthen virtue. These he describe as generosity, moral restraint and meditation.

The Four Noble Truths (on day 14) given by Peter Friedlander as 'Dukkha, the arising of Dukkha, the cessation of Dukkha, and a path to the cessation of Dukkha.' (Buddhism Past and Present p62) Dukkha is loosely translated as suffering and Goldstein points out the truth and causes of this suffering, as well as the path that leads to it's ending.

Karma (on day 16) which he describes as the 'law of cause and effect…. Each action produces a certain result' (TEOI p97) He then goes on to discuss how Karma acts in our lives.

Dependent Origination (on day 21) which is a linked 'chain' binding us to the wheel of life, death and rebirth. The links are given by Peter Harvey as: 1/ Spiritual ignorance > 2 / Constructing activities > 3/ (discriminative) Consciousness > 4/ Mind-and-body > 5/ The six senses > 7/ Feeling > 8/ Craving > 9/ Grasping > 10/ Existence > 11/ Birth > 12/ Ageing, death, sorrow etc. ('An introduction to Buddhism' p55) According to Goldstein this chain can be broken by using 'powerful mindfulness' and 'not clinging' so that we can overcome desire and grasping and thus avoid the volitional activity of becoming. 'Every moment of awareness is a hammer stroke on this chain of conditioning.' (TEOI p120)

2/ Direct Meditation Instructions where Goldstein gives advice on dealing with:

Feelings (on day 3) where the instruction is to be mindful physical sensations without clinging to or identifying with them.

Thoughts (on day 5) where he says 'simply be aware, as thoughts rise, that the mind is thinking without getting involved in the content' (TEOI p27)

Sense objects (on day 6): here he urges that we just be aware of sensations (caused by sense objects) arising and passing away, then return to breath awareness.

Intentions (on day 8), about which he advises that we should be mindful in sitting, walking and changing posture. This leads to 'insight into the interrelated way mind-body processes work.' As this develops 'the concept of self dissolves into a simple and natural unfolding of the elements.' (TEOI p48)

Eating (on day 9), where the instruction is to eat mindfully, seeing the food (and the intention to eat it), and remain mindful during every process of eating, thus turning it into a meditation.

Consciousness (on day 10), which he defines as 'the knowing facility' which is a function of the mind. Here one has to be careful to distinguish this from the way it is Upanishadically defined which is akin to 'pure awareness' which is deeper than, or behind, the mind. Goldstein suggests that we remain mindful of, or investigate, this knowing of the mind in order to discover that there is in truth no-one who observes or witnesses.

Relaxing/Sinking Mind (on day 17) where he discusses resolving not to move during meditation sessions, and when pain arises relaxing the whole body letting go of the reaction to the pain. There is also a warning against sinking into a pleasant dreamlike state. The aim is to stay watchful and attentive.

3/ General Buddhist Thought/Information and Stories.

In the remaining fourteen talks Goldstein explores a wide range of Buddhist thought including: bare attention, concepts and reality, hindrances, concentration, resolution, purity, happiness, devotion, death, loving kindness, enlightenment and Buddhist paths. He also tells various stories and talks about 'the warrior', the Tao, St. John of the Cross and St Francis de Sales. It is beyond the scope of this essay to elaborate further on these topics. Suffice it to say that they are designed to 'fill in the gaps' left by Buddha's philosophy and Goldstein's instructions. They also give illustrations as to how this Buddhist path relates to Taoism and certain Christian mystics.

Finally, in closing, on the last day he discusses the integration of meditation and its practice into everyday life. He urges us to stay mindful and 'sit' at set times twice a day. He suggests that walking can be used as a meditation as on the retreat. He also advises that we keep in mind the truth of impermanence, and that we cultivate love, compassion and humility (or 'invisibility'). 'Empty your boat, go through life in an open, empty and loving way' (TEOI p168).

Summing up I would say that 'The Experience of Insight' is indeed ' A Simple and Direct Guide to Meditation' relating to the particular meditational techniques that he espouses. He gives us complete instructions in the techniques of these meditations and ways to deal with any problems that may occur. He backs this up with explaining Buddha's philosophy which he expands with much information about Theravadan Buddhist thought. There are also many question/answer sections which help clarify the text and stories which enliven it. All in all I would say that if you wish to practice this form of Vipassana meditation you could not do better than Goldstein's book.

Twenty – The Missing Steps

Proposes that Vipassana meditation does not go far enough as it does not address the question of self-identity - 'who am I'? Further Tibetan and Zen breath awareness meditation, which does address this, fails to consider the function of human beings as expressions, and instruments of, The Absolute.

From my point of view Vipassana is a method to allow one to see that all things are transitory, Annica – impermanence, and that there exists no separate self, Annatta – no Atman (Self). These are key Buddhist concepts, but further steps are required as I pointed out in the previous chapter:

> Breathing in, he knows breathing in, hearing a sound he knows hearing, smelling a smell he knows smelling, thought arising he knows thinking." … attributed to The Buddha. This is awareness of what is occurring through (or to) the body/mind, a small step away from seeing that these breaths, sounds, smells, thoughts etc occur in Awareness itself, for he is aware of them. Which is then 'awareness of Awareness' for he is then noticing (aware of) Awareness itself, and just effortlessly resting in that 'seeing' is 'relaxing into awareness of Awareness'.

This is what Vipassana fails to address, that behind the mind seeing (aware of) thoughts and sensations there is the Pure Awareness - the constant, conscious subjective presence – in which these arise, abide, are spied and subside. This is akin to seeing the 'ripples on the lake of Awareness' and not identifying with them, for they are transitory, but not seeing the lake itself. This is not totally satisfactory as - although it negates all clinging, for there is truly nothing to cling to, and no-one to cling - it does not address the inescapable feeling that 'I am', that is to say it does not answer the question 'who am I?' This is undoubtedly what I found to be disappointing when I went to my first, and only, Vipassana retreat, for I find correct identification with the essence of what one **is** to be the key to liberation. For more on this see appendix one 'Investigation of Experience' which addresses all of these points.

This is addressed in Mahayana Buddhism as the following from *Beyond The Separate Self* shows:

> As Buddhism developed and spread, it evolved the Tibetan (Buddhist) concept of Rigpa or 'Ground Luminosity' and the Zen idea of 'Universal Mind'. Both of these concepts are equivalent to the 'pure consciousness' or 'awareness' in which all appears, exists and disappears. About Rigpa, Sogyal Rinpoche says, 'In Tibetan we call it Rigpa, a primordial, pure, pristine awareness that is at once intelligent, cognizant, radiant and always awake …. It is in fact the nature of everything'.[29] Dudjon Rinpoche adds, 'It has never been born, been liberated, been deluded, existed, been nonexistent, it has no limits and falls into no category'.[30] Padmasambhava, the founder of Tibetan Buddhism in 775AD,[31] described Rigpa as:
>
> > The self-originated Clear Light which … was never born. It has never experienced birth and nothing could

---

[29] S. Rinpoche *The Tibetan Book of Living and Dying*, 1992, San Francisco, p. 47
[30] Ibid. p. 49
[31] P. Harvey, *Buddhism*, 1990, Cambridge, p. 145

cause it to die … although it is evidently visible, yet there is no one who sees it … Although it exists in everyone everywhere it has gone unrecognized.[32]

According to *The Tibetan Book of the Dead* Rigpa is the first thing one encounters after death: 'The nature of everything is open, empty and naked like the sky, luminous emptiness without centre or circumference; the pure naked Rigpa dawns'.[33]

Universal or Big Mind is the name used by the Zen school whose 'founding genius was seen as the semi-legendary Indian monk Bodhidharma … active in China between 470 to 520 AD'.[34] About this 'Mind' he is recorded as saying:

> Only the wise know this Mind, this Mind called *dharma* nature, this Mind called liberation. Neither life nor death can restrain this Mind. Nothing can. It's also called the unstoppable *Tagatha*, the Incomprehensible, the Sacred Self, the Immortal, the Great Sage … The Mind's capacity is limitless and its manifestations are inexhaustible … The Mind has no form and its awareness no limit.[35]

---

[32] S. Rinpoche *The Tibetan Book of Living and Dying,* 1992, San Francisco, p. 260
[33] Ibid. p. 259
[34] P. Harvey, '*Buddhism*', 1990, Cambridge, p. 153
[35] S. Rajneesh, '*Bodhidharma*', 1987, Cologne, p. 71-72

We find this Zen Mind also described in '*Zen Mind, Beginner's Mind*' by Shunryu Suzuki as something which is 'always with you', 'watching mind' and 'our true Buddha nature'. He also talks about small 'I' and big 'I' and our 'true self'. Finally, he says, 'You should be able to appreciate things as an expression of big Mind '. [36]

Thus the Theravada School, which sticks to Buddha's original teachings, remain quiet on the existence or non-existence of the Absolute but does admit a supra-mundane state of *nirvana*, whilst the Mahayana schools of Tibetan and Zen Buddhism do accept an Absolute reality whose nature is of pure awareness or consciousness.[37]

And this from *Freedom From Anxiety and Needless Suffering*:

Firstly considering why we practice meditation. On page 59 of *The Tibetan Book of Living and Dying* (hereafter denoted by 'TB") we find:

The purpose of meditation is to awaken in us the sky-like nature of mind, and to introduce us to that which we

---

[36] S. Suzuki, 'Zen Mind, Beginners' Mind', 1970, New York, p. 134-137
[37] C.Drake, *Beyond The Separate Self,* 2009, Tomewin, p. 137-139

really are, our unchanging pure awareness, which underlies the whole of life and death.

Then on page 21 of Zen *Mind, Beginners Mind* (hereafter called 'ZM') Suzuki says:

The goal of practice is always to keep our beginners (original) mind... Our 'original mind' includes everything within itself. It is always rich and sufficient within itself.

Although the terminology is different both Sogyal Rinpoche (hereafter denoted by 'SR') and Shunryu Suzuki (hereafter denoted by 'SS') are talking about the same thing. 'Pure awareness' and 'original mind' are that in which all things appear, exist and disappear; that 'which underlies the whole of life and death' and 'includes everything within itself'. So the aim of meditation is to realize our true, inner nature as 'pure awareness or 'original mind'. As SR continues (on p.59 TB): 'In the stillness and silence of meditation we glimpse and return to that deep inner nature'. Which SS confirms (on p.23 ZM): 'Zazen (meditation) practice is the direct expression of our true nature'.[38]

---

[38] C.Drake, *Freedom Form Anxiety and Needless Suffering,* 2015, Tomewin, p. 103-104

So Vipassana meditation, from the Theravadan school, does not answer the question 'who am I?' whereas breath awareness meditation in Tibetan and Zen Buddhism does. However even these do not go one step further and consider the function of a human being as an expression and instrument of Pure Awareness, its 'true nature', see appendix two 'Instruments of The Absolute'.

Which is a great pity for the tendency of many teachings to denigrate the mind and body, resulting in limiting the scope of the mind and a life constricted by renunciation, causes them to miss a range of important opportunities presented by being in a physical body. Which is not surprising, as they have failed to realize the potential of the body/mind as an instrument through which The Absolute can know, enjoy and love its manifestation. An example of this is the following exchange between me and my lecturer on Buddhism at Latrobe University when I asked him to give the Buddhist viewpoint on my comment:

> Myself - That all living things are instruments of this awareness through which it (Pure Awareness – Consciousness) interacts with and enjoys its manifestation.

> Lecturer - No answer to that question. Sounds like an echo of samsara and lila to me. Not normally a Buddhist pair of concepts, as it appears to impute volition to pure awareness, which is not a viewpoint held by any Buddhist school I know of.

This answer is not surprising given that the Buddha refused to answer questions on the existence of an Absolute Reality regarding them as irrelevant in the undertaking of overcoming suffering. Here is a quote on this from chapter twenty of *Beyond The Separate Self*:

> As far as answering questions on The Absolute, Buddha regarded all such questions as unconnected with the goal of overcoming suffering and achieving *nirvana*. In his famous discourse with the sage Malunkyaputta he likened this to a man who, being pierced with an arrow, spending his time questioning the type, make, source and firer of the arrow, rather than just pulling it out.[39]

While the realization of body/mind as an instrument may not be necessary to overcome suffering, it certainly is to nurture the full potential of physicality and to honour Consciousness and Its manifestation. Moreover, correct identification of oneself as (and with) Pure Awareness (Consciousness at rest) is the quickest method to overcome unnecessary suffering and existential angst, plus having many other wonderful benefits detailed in various chapters of my books.

So the Theravadans do not consider the question 'who am I?' and both they and the Mahayanists overlook the function of, and the joy of using,

[39] I. B. Homer, 'Cula-Malunkyasutta', 1989, Oxford, p97-101

the body/mind as an expression and instrument of Pure Awareness. Once again see appendices one and two.

Twenty One – Love and Knowledge

This chapter discusses how the 'paths' of knowledge, Jnana Yoga, and love, Bhakti Yoga, lead to the same result.

The approaches, to the divine, of knowledge and love can both have the same outcome which is to go beyond the illusory 'separate self' and realize the Universal Self, Consciousness, in which all arises, abides, is spied and subsides. The former uses investigation and reasoning to realize that, at a deeper level than body/mind, there exists Pure Awareness which is the seer, source and dissolution of all sensation and thought. Whereas, in the latter love for the divine, in whatever form, eventually becomes so strong that there is total self-surrender which entails the loss of the separate self. That is not to say that these are exclusively different 'paths' as an example of how the former can lead to the latter, that is knowledge to love, consider the following from *Beyond The Separate Self*:

> A study of the world's religions reveals two major themes concerning the purpose of creation and the function of humanity. It is suggested that the Absolute, Consciousness at rest (Pure Awareness), created (or manifested as) the universe for Its enjoyment and so that It could know Itself. For when Consciousness is totally at rest It has no objects to be aware of, and thus no form of experience is possible; so the only way for any enjoyment to occur is for the 'potential energy', latent in the Absolute, to manifest into cosmic energy and thus the universe. Then instruments are needed to 'sense' this manifestation, so that these sensations appear in Awareness, which is the function of all conscious organisms.

As far as 'knowing Itself', It needs some form of mechanism, such as the human mind, which is capable of self-recognition; and this is what occurs when we realize our deeper level of being which is this Pure Awareness itself. For this realization appears in the mind and thus in Awareness itself. Thus the human mind/body has the function of attaining self-realization and enjoying existence in order that the purpose of creation is fulfilled. This enjoyment of existence is greatly enhanced by seeing and experiencing the world 'as it is', that is by encountering it totally and directly, rather than through the filter of the mind. This occurs only when we identify at the deeper level than body/mind so that the mind's opinions, judgements, interpretations, etc. are seen for what they are, ephemeral thoughts coming and going in awareness itself. As one deepens one's identification with Pure Awareness the mind stills and then the world is encountered directly, with 'no mind', and is experienced as it truly 'is'. A Hindu term for the Absolute is *Satchitananda*, which can be translated as: *Sat*-'what is' (the manifestation), *chit*- the awareness of 'what is', *ananda*- the bliss of the awareness of 'what is'.

In fact once one relaxes into pure awareness one can actually feel the bliss of embodiment through the sensations in the body, a subtle throbbing of the life force, and through that which is detected by the other senses. This bliss is present in every moment and can be detected by bringing one's whole attention to the sensation in question, without any 'second thought' about the sensation and what it could mean or without relating it to any 'story' of oneself. This culminates into being totally in love with the whole of existence, a love where the beloved is always present as there is no separation between the lover and the beloved. The lover being the deeper level of Pure Awareness, Consciousness at rest, and the beloved being the surface level of manifestation, Consciousness in motion. In this context *Satchitananda* becomes: *Sat* –the beloved, *chit*- the lover beholding the beloved, *ananda* - the bliss of the lover beholding the beloved.

The corollary to this is that when one achieves self-realization, recognizing that at a deeper level one is Pure Awareness, then this is the beloved beholding the lover. The beloved being the surface level of mind/body, the manifestation, realizing the deeper level of Consciousness at rest, the lover. This completes the cycle of the Absolute using the mind/body to sense, experience, interact with and enjoy its manifestation, and also to recognize (or 'know') Itself.[40]

---

[40] C.Drake, *Beyond The Separate Self*, 2009, Tomewin, p.113-115

With regard to how the path of worship, love, leads to self-surrender, and thus loss of the separate self, here is a previous article on the subject:

Worship and Realization

Discusses how worship can result in the same self-realization as the discovery that, at the deepest level, we are The Absolute Reality - Pure Awareness- Consciousness at rest. Sri Ramakrishna is quoted for he discovered this experientially, worshipping many different Hindu deities and following the path of 'knowledge' (Jnana Yoga) and finding that they all lead to the same conclusion.

This article attempts to show how worship, even of images, which is so prevalent in Hinduism, leads to the same realization as correctly identifying oneself with the True Self – Pure Awareness, Consciousness at rest in which all (motion) arises, abides and subsides. The approach I have taken uses the word 'image' in its broadest sense to show why Hindus regard the whole of creation to be sacred, a divine manifestation; which ties in with the fact that all manifestation is composed of Cosmic Energy – Consciousness (the divine) in motion. This helps to explain the way they image/worship the divine in not only gods/goddesses but also in nature such as rivers, mountains, trees etc. For this I shall use the great mystic, of the late 19th century, Sri Ramakrishna as my source. Here was a semi-literate man who

approached the divine in many different ways through the worship of
Kali the divine mother, Siva which denotes the Absolute (Brahman -
Consciousness), Krishna and Rama, who are regarded as incarnations of
Vishnu, the preserving aspect of Brahman. He also practiced Tantra,
which uses the totality of human experience to approach the divine, and
Advaita Vedanta which aims for divine union by negating all
manifestation as Maya (illusion). In his own experience he found that
all these sadhanas (spiritual practices) yielded the same experience of
divine union although travelling on vastly different paths. He likened it
to climbing a mountain by many different paths all of which eventually
reached the summit.

This summit, or ground of being, is Brahman the Absolute, the
Supreme Reality. About this he says "Nothing exists except the One.
That One is the Supreme Brahman. So long as he keeps the I in us, He
reveals to us that it is He who as the Primal Energy, creates, preserves
and destroys the universe." (The Gospel of Ramakrishna p 242)
Generally the name Brahman is used when the absolute is inactive
(Pure Awareness – Consciousness at rest) and Sakti, or Kali is used for
the Cosmic Energy- Consciousness in motion. Ramakrishna
worshipped Kali as Sakti, this divine energy which creates preserves
and destroys the universe. These aspects are also personified as
Brahma the creator, Vishnu the preserver and Siva the destroyer. Note
that Siva is also regarded as denoting the Absolute, in that once all

manifestation has been destroyed only the Absolute remains. Ramakrishna states that:

> Brahman and Sakti are identical. The Primordial Power is ever
> at play. When we think of it as inactive, that is to say not
> engaged in the acts of creation, preservation and destruction, the
> we call it Brahman. But when it engages in those activities we
> call it Kali or Sakti. The Reality is one and the same
> [Consciousness]; the difference is in name and form. (The
> Gospel of Ramakrishna p 134-135)

> There are two schools of thought the Vedanta and the Purana.
> According to the Vedanta the world is illusory like a dream.
> But according to the Purana God himself has become the twenty
> four cosmic principles[41]. Worship God both within and without.
> As long as God keeps the awareness of 'I' in us so long do sense
> objects exist and we cannot very well speak of the world as a
> dream. (The Gospel of Ramakrishna p 243)

The implication is that as long as any sense of identification prevails (even as an instrument of Pure Awareness) one should see all things as manifestations of the divine. Once all identification has been transcended, by realizing that no separate self exists, the One (Consciousness) is revealed and every thing in manifestation can be regarded as 'illusory' – that is ephemeral and having no inherent

[41] 'The twenty four cosmic principles' denotes all of creation.

existence as a separate object. All deities are aspects of the one Absolute Reality. About this Ramakrishna says: "In the same way some address the Reality as 'Allah' some as 'God' some as 'Brahman' some as 'Kali' and others by such names as Rama, Jesus, Durga, Hari." (The Gospel of Ramakrishna p 135)

These statements are not just intellectual knowledge but were actual realizations of his many sadhanas which also include following Christianity and Islam. So the many different gods and goddesses in Hinduism represent different aspects of the absolute Brahman/Kali, Purusha/Prakriti, Rama/Sita, Krishna/Radha, call it what you will..... Generally the divine energy was considered to be feminine and the absolute masculine, in all of the previous cases the first name is that denoting the Absolute (Pure Awareness – Consciousness at rest) and the second the divine energy (motion in Consciousness or Consciousness in motion) which derives from, resides in and subsides back into the Absolute; for all motion arises from stillness, exists in a substratum of stillness and finally returns to stillness ...

The point is that whichever sadhana you perform, or whichever god/goddess or natural phenomenon you worship, if you follow the practice with dedication, self-surrender, and perseverance until finally you completely lose yourself (losing all identification as a separate being) you will experience the same divine union with the Absolute.

Or, more accurately, you will realise that you are, and have never been separate from, the Absolute – Consciousness Itself.[42]

---

[42] C.Drake, *Freedom From Anxiety and Needless Suffering*, 2015, Tomewin, p. 122-126

Twenty Two – Love is All There Is

This chapter posits that 'love is no separation' and in the Absolute (Consciousness at rest and in motion, which is all there is) there is no separation and thus love.

Fully requited love requires 'no separation', that is to be forever with the beloved, in spirit if not in form. In fact 'no separation' is a valid definition of the ultimate love, for more on this see 'Love is No Separation' in *Awakening and Beyond*, from which the following has been taken:

> To see this we need to start by defining 'Love', which I am going to give as 'empathetic attraction' (for or to). Then its various names, associated with different types, will indicate its nature in terms of strength, commitment, attachment, etc.

> This definition 'empathetic attraction' implies being attracted to, and thus wishing to be in the presence of, one with whom one empathises. So that this means being attracted to someone with whom we can identify and so 'fully comprehend'.[43] This gives the clue that to attain universal love (agape) we must be able to identify with everyone we encounter. To do this we must be able to view every person as of the same essence, pure awareness, and thus realize that there is essentially no difference between oneself and anyone else. In this case we can fully comprehend the essence of what it is to be human without needing to fully comprehend everyone's individual character traits.

---

[43] *Australian Pocket Oxford Dictionary*, 2002, S. Melbourne p.359

This implies that there is no separation between oneself and another. From this follows that one would naturally treat others as oneself (or as one would wish to be treated by others) … which is itself a pretty good definition of brotherly (universal) love.

It could be argued that this (agape) is the 'coolest' form of love, but can this definition of love as 'no separation' be applied to all forms of love, especially the 'hottest' eros which is 'passionate and committed'? To consider this I can only rely on my two personal experiences of being deeply in love. In both cases I longed to be with my beloved at all times … in a state of 'no separation', and was only happy when in her presence. This is borne out by literature, drama, films and pop-culture all of which emphasise this aspect of 'love'. So if 'no separation' can be applied to the coolest and hottest forms of love I would argue that it must also be applicable to all forms in between.

At the experiential level, once awakening has taken place, then there can be a deep feeling of not being separate from one's environment or any other being. In my case this has been accompanied by being 'in love with existence', here is what I wrote about this during my first 'awakening' at a silent retreat in 1996:

The best way to describe the feeling that accompanies all of this is as being deeply in love with a beloved who is always present, both within and without. It was even accompanied by some of the physical symptoms I experienced the first time I fell deeply in love, a deep throbbing of the heart, queasiness of the stomach and an overall glow and sense of well-being.[44]

So based on all of the above I posit that 'Love is no separation'.

In universal terms the manifestation, Cosmic Energy – Consciousness in motion (the beloved) is never separate from Pure Awareness – Consciousness at rest (the lover). The Absolute – Consciousness exists in both of these 'modes', which are never separate from It, and thus exists in a state of no separation, which is Love. I put this in both human and universal terms into a poem for a questioner who asked for 'proof':

You ask for proof,
What more proof could there be?
That which lives and breathes in me,
Also lives and breathes in thee.

The Lover and Beloved are ever within and without,
Of this amazing Mystery there can be no doubt.

---

[44] C. Drake, *Beyond the Separate Self,* 2009, Halifax, p.183-184

She feels every sensation that our bodies feel,
As we eat She partakes of every meal.

That which we hear and see,
Is also heard and seen by the Beloved, Thee.
All that we taste and smell,
Is sensed, through us, by Thee as well.

Every thought with which our minds resound,
In Thy infinite Cosmic Mind is found.
For behind every conscious body/mind,
The Seer, Knower and Enjoyer can we find.

In this there can be no separate 'saying',
Manifestation is the Lover and Beloved playing.
What appears to us as 'you' and 'me',
Are expressions, and instruments, of the Beloved, Thee.

Between Awareness and the Creation,
There can be no separation.
For the Lover and Beloved are always one,
Appearing as the 'many' just for fun!

As there is no separation between the lover and beloved then these are forever united in love and, in this total unity, you could say that 'all is (in) love' or that 'love is (encompasses) all there is'. For love requires consciousness and unity, and all is Consciousness in motion or at rest. As all motion arises from, abides in and subsides back into stillness, then in this there is unity (no separation) and thus love, which encompasses all.

♫"Love is all there is" …

"Love is all there is" …

"Love is all there is" …♫

Twenty Three - Nurturing The Bliss of Awakening

The next three chapters are devoted to love of the Absolute, the source, by Its manifestation and to love of Its manifestation by the Absolute. In this discussion the Absolute, Consciousness at rest, is called 'the lover' and the manifestation 'the beloved'. In the first of these chapters deals with concentrating on, and enjoying/loving, one sensation – that of feelings in, and on the surface, of the body. The following chapter expands this to focussing on all of the five senses one by one. Finally the third deals with noticing all of the senses together, sequentially laying them 'on top' of each other.

In a recent article 'Love Loving Itself' (next chapter) I described a method for experiencing the Absolute (Pure Awareness – Consciousness at rest – the deepest level of our being - the lover) loving the beloved (the manifestation – Consciousness in motion) using the physical body as its instrument for this. I have recently discovered that if one lengthens this practice, concentrating on the subtle bliss of embodiment then the mind becomes still and the bliss slowly increases …

If you like light some subtle incense to add to the atmosphere in the room and brush your teeth (or eat something pleasant) to ensure that there is an agreeable taste in the mouth. Make sure that the phone is on silent and that the 'do not disturb' sign is on the door.

Lie, or sit, in the <u>most comfortable position you can possibly find</u>, with your eyes closed. I would recommend Shavasana (the corpse pose) lying flat on your back with your legs slightly apart, feet falling gently outwards, and your arms slightly away from the body with your palms facing upwards. Do this on a bed, couch, or soft carpet with a cushion or pillow under the head. If you are cold or hot then adjust your clothing/covering until your temperature is perfect. If you are in pain then take a pain killer an hour before this practice, or if in great pain then, if possible, vary your pain management strategy until no pain is present. The point is to adjust your circumstances, if possible, to the point where there is absolutely no discomfort.

So now lying in absolute comfort, notice that Awareness is always present and that it is very easy to see that for this to be the case there is absolutely nothing the mind needs to do. Similarly there is no problem that the mind needs to solve to recognize this deeper level of Awareness, as this very Awareness is never absent, being the constant conscious presence in which all thoughts and sensations appear. For without this presence we would not be aware of any thought or sensation.[45] Also, as this is the only constant factor that has been present throughout (and witnessed) our entire lives, whereas our thoughts/sensations (mind/bodies) are always changing, then this Awareness is what we truly are at the most fundamental level.

So now, there being nothing to achieve, find or acquire, one can totally 'let go' and relax deeply into this Awareness …

Now notice the sensations (and feelings) in, and on the surface of, the body. Sink into these sensations, really luxuriate in them as much as possible. Ignore all other sense impressions and thoughts except these sensations. Realize that these occur, are detected by the nervous system, processed by the brain and are then 'seen' by Awareness – i.e. you become 'aware' of them.

---

[45] From *Beyond The Separate Self* p.85

179

So the body/mind (itself a manifestation of cosmic energy – the beloved) is an instrument through which Awareness- Consciousness at rest, the lover – can feel the external world – Consciousness in motion, the beloved.

If this is continued with for some time one starts to feel the bliss of embodiment – the rhythmic beating of the heart, the blood pumping through the veins, the air on one's face, the warmth in one's feet, sensations of the touching points where the body is in contact with the ground (cushion, pillow, mattress etc.) and so on. The more one can sink into, and luxuriate in, these sensations the stronger the practice becomes.

Just continue with this luxuriating, aware of the fact that this is Awareness itself (Consciousness at rest – the lover), which is what in essence you are, using the body/mind as a medium to feel Its manifestation the physical world – cosmic energy – Consciousness in motion – the beloved. Thus the lover is able to sense its own manifestation – the beloved.

The bliss can be quite subtle at first, so if you are not aware of this then start with the feeling of ease and comfort as the body sinks more deeply into its support. Notice the absolute freedom of nothing to achieve, seek for or desire, as That which you could want is always already here – Pure Awareness itself! First focus on the touching points where the body comes into contact with its supporting surface. Deeply feel the sensation of letting go into this and the relaxation and comfort associated with this. Then come to the effortless rising and falling of the chest and abdomen as your body gently calmly breathes itself … feel the ease of this for some time. Next notice the soft caress of your shirt, or blouse, as your chest and abdomen move up into and then down away from this. Feel the gentle joy of all this for a period before becoming aware of the slightly cooling air on the face and hands and then of the subtle throbbing of the circulation as the blood flows around the body.

If thoughts arise just let them come and go whilst simply returning to this balmy bliss of being in the body. As the practice continues these thoughts will lessen, especially if you remain identified with this Awareness which is witnessing all of the bodily sensations as they ebb and they flow. Also, the mind will find it easy to return to the bliss, as this will be 'tastier' than any thoughts which arise and the mind is programmed to seek for pleasure. This will lead to the bliss slowly magnifying as the distractions lessen and the sensations will seem to intensify as you become more deeply aware of them.

Continue this for as long as you are comfortable and you can mentally repeat 'feeling you my love' with each 'wave' of sensation, or with the breath, if this appeals to you. For you are indeed the 'lover' (Pure Awareness – Consciousness at rest) feeling the 'beloved' - Its manifestation, the universe, cosmic energy, Consciousness in motion. For this the body/mind is a wonderful instrument with its extensive nervous system (system of nerves which pervade the whole body) and other senses. Alternatively, you can mentally repeat 'the bliss of the beloved' as you feel the ease and comfort of these sensations, which I find slowly increases the bliss as it is repeated. I suspect that there is an increase of endorphin release during this whole process which is also stimulated by the continual mental repetition of the words 'love' or 'bliss'. It is well known that mind states affect the bodily functions (and feelings) and I posit that this is a classic example of this occurring. At all events the bliss increases as the mind stills and the utter relaxation deepens…

As you arise, from this practice of deeply blissful relaxation, take your time slowly 'coming to' and try to maintain this 'loving feeling' towards your surroundings for as long as possible. Then:

When awake we can feel the bliss,

Of living, which we generally miss.

Resulting in loving one and all,

On whomsoe'er one's eye may fall[46].

---

[46] From *Poetry From Beyond The Separate Self, The Best of All Worlds* p.69

This is a classic win-win situation where the mind is engaged doing something it finds to be easy and really enjoys, whilst revealing that the mind/body is indeed a conduit through which Awareness can enjoy Its own manifestation. There is also no referencing to an illusory 'individual self' as identifying with, and as, Pure Awareness is the prerequisite to commencing (and staying engaged in) the whole practice.

The results of this will eventually permeate your entire day so this bliss may be readily re-accessed at any time by sitting, or lying, quietly and bringing your attention to it. It also makes seemingly stressful situations less so, as the underlying bliss (or peace) negates the negative emotions as they attempt to arise; or even prevents them arising at all!

To give a personal example of this:
I am an Englishman who has now been living in Australia for over forty years … what luck! However, as I was from a cool to cold climate I am not keen on very hot weather and tended to overheat (physically and then mentally) quite easily when the mercury rises above 30C (86F) and I am working outside. Luckily (my life is full of this) I am self-employed in an indoor occupation and the pottery is shady and cool even on the hottest days. So, when I have outdoor work to do, we have an old macadamia plantation over 10 acres, I normally choose cool days for this. Yesterday, however, our old campervan chose not to start so I called the local roadside assistance for help. By the time he arrived at

midday it was 35C (95F) in the shade and over 40C (104F) in the sun. We spent over an hour and a half outside (with no shade) attempting to start and then towing the van out. It was parked under the kiln-shelter, down an exposed narrow drive with steep sides, which contains a 150 degree bend, and was thus very tricky to extricate. I noticed that, although I did get very hot physically, I stayed calm and cheerful throughout the whole process … which would have been impossible before my awakening and the subsequent cultivation of this.

I also accepted the fact that our seven day trip, to various 'highland' national parks, would have to be abandoned, without any resistance … actually I went home, cooled down, and then did a yoga-nidra. This is a very powerful relaxation technique which my wife and I have been doing, on a daily basis, for over 30 years and which can change (in fact is guaranteed to after enough practice) one's head space from agitated to serene in less than half an hour. In fact, this has many similarities with the practice I have outlined above, although it has other components and does not focus on the bliss.[47]

---

[47] C.Drake, *The Simplicity of Awakening*, 2015, Tomewin, p. 107-114

Twenty Four – Love Loving Itself

This chapter expands on the previous one by becoming aware of, and enjoying, all of the five senses one at a time. This leads to the lover loving the beloved, which is then reversed by using the mind (a facet of the beloved) to investigate Awareness (the lover) Itself. The result of this is that the beloved gets to 'know' and love the lover. So that the whole practice is one by which the lover and beloved can 'know' and love each other. Or to put it another way by which Consciousness can 'know' and love Itself in both 'modes' when at rest (as Pure Awareness) and when in motion (as Its manifestation).

This is a powerful practice for 'sensing' The Absolute, in which there is no reference to the imaginary separate self. I recommended this to a reader who was continually beset with his own 'story' and here is the outcome:

Hi Colin,

I'm doing beautifully since I seriously started doing the "Love Loving Itself" exercise several times a day. I'm not certain precisely when a "shift" occurred, but my true nature as Awareness is now perceived with much greater clarity and consistency than the endless and unmerciful "story of me".

Ironically, this truth has been what I am since my very birth, right in front of my nose!

With Love and Thanks,

XXXX

Here is the practice, through which the lover - pure Awareness, consciousness at rest – and the beloved – the manifest universe, cosmic energy, consciousness in motion – can 'know' and love each other. Thus The Absolute, consciousness in both modes, can know and love Itself.

Lie, or sit, in the most comfortable position you can possibly find, with your eyes closed. Make sure that the phone is off the hook and that the 'do not disturb' sign is on the door.

1/ Notice the sensations (and feelings) in, and on the surface of, the body. Sink into these sensations, really luxuriate in them as much as possible. Ignore all other sense impressions and thoughts except these sensations.

(If it appeals you may mentally repeat *Feeling you my love* as you do this.)

Realize that these occur, are detected by the nervous system, and are then 'seen' by Awareness – i.e. you become 'aware' of them.

So the body/mind is an instrument through which Awareness-consciousness at rest, the lover – can feel the external world – consciousness in motion, the beloved.

2/ Notice the sounds, occurring in the body and the room. Ignore all other sense impressions and thoughts except these sounds.

(If it appeals you may mentally repeat *Hearing you my love* as you do this.)

Realize that these occur, are detected by the ears, and are then 'seen' by Awareness – i.e. you become 'aware' of them.

So the body/mind is an instrument through which Awareness-consciousness at rest, the lover – can hear the external world – consciousness in motion, the beloved.

3/ Notice the aromas occurring in the room. Ignore all other sense impressions and thoughts except these aromas.

(If it appeals you may mentally repeat *Smelling you my love* as you do this.)

Realize that these occur, are detected by the nose, and are then 'seen' by Awareness – i.e. you become 'aware' of them.

So the body/mind is an instrument through which Awareness-consciousness at rest, the lover – can smell the external world – consciousness in motion, the beloved.

4/ Notice the tastes, occurring in the mouth. Ignore all other sense impressions and thoughts except these tastes.

(If it appeals you may mentally repeat *Tasting you my love* as you do this.)

Realize that these occur, are detected by the taste buds, and are then 'seen' by Awareness – i.e. you become 'aware' of them.

So the body/mind is an instrument through which Awareness-consciousness at rest, the lover – can taste the external world – consciousness in motion, the beloved.

5/ Open your eyes and notice what is seen. Ignore all other sense impressions and thoughts except these sights.

(If it appeals you may mentally repeat *Seeing you my love* as you do this.)

Realize that these occur, are detected by the eye, and are then 'seen' by Awareness – i.e. you become 'aware' of them.
So the body/mind is an instrument through which Awareness-consciousness at rest, the lover – can see the external world – consciousness in motion, the beloved.

6/ Close your eyes and notice the thoughts, occurring in the mind. Ignore all sense impressions just noticing the thoughts.

(If it appeals you may mentally repeat *Thinking of you my love* as you do this.)

Realize that these occur, are detected by the mind, and are then 'seen' by Awareness – i.e. you become 'aware' of them.

So the body/mind is an instrument through which Awareness-consciousness at rest, the lover – can contemplate the external world – consciousness in motion, the beloved.

7/ Notice the mental images occurring in the mind. Ignore all sense impressions just noticing these images.
(If it appeals you may mentally repeat *Imagining you my love* as you do this.)
Realize that these occur, are detected by the mind, and are then 'seen' by Awareness – i.e. you become 'aware' of them.

So the body/mind is an instrument through which Awareness-consciousness at rest, the lover – can imagine the external world – consciousness in motion, the beloved.

8/ Therefore the body/mind is an instrument through which Awareness-consciousness at rest, the lover – can experience, engage with and enjoy the external world – consciousness in motion, the beloved.

9/ To put this another way the body/mind – itself an ephemeral manifestation of consciousness in motion, the beloved – is an instrument, or conduit, through which the lover can 'know' and love the beloved.

This is the end of the first phase, that of the lover loving the beloved.

10/ Now notice that through this practice you are 'aware of Awareness'. This means that the mind notices the presence of Awareness. So this is the beloved noticing the lover.

Next investigate this Awareness so that the beloved can 'get to know' the lover better:

11/ Observe whether any effort is required to be aware of any thought/mental image/sensation.

This readily reveals that this Awareness is effortlessly present and effortlessly aware... It requires no effort by the mind/body and they cannot make it vanish however much effort they apply.

12/ Observe whether there is any choice in becoming aware of thoughts/mental images/sensations.

This also reveals that this Awareness is choicelessly present and choicelessly aware. Once again, it requires no choice of the body/mind and they cannot block it however they try. i.e. If you have a toothache there is effortless Awareness of it and the mind/body cannot choose for this not to be the case. You may think that this is bad news but that is not the case, can you imagine if you had to make a choice whether you would like to be aware for every sensation that the body experiences! In fact be grateful that there is no effort or choice involved for Awareness just to be...such ease and simplicity...which is not surprising for, at the deepest level, you are this Awareness!

13/ Observe whether you can ever experience a time or place when Awareness is not present. Even during sleep there is Awareness of dreams, the quality of the sleep, and bodily sensations, in that if a noise is loud enough or a feeling (of pain or discomfort for instance) is strong enough it will bring the mind back to the conscious state, i.e. One will wake up... The natural conclusion to this is that for each of us Awareness is omnipresent, i.e. always present. Once again be grateful that the mind/body is never required to search for this Awareness, it is just always there, which of course is not surprising for one is this Awareness.

14/ Next notice that this Awareness is absolutely still for it is aware of the slightest movement of body or mind. For example we all know that to be completely 'aware' of what is going on around us in a busy environment we have to be completely still, just witnessing the activity.

15/ In the same vein this Awareness can be 'seen' to be totally silent as it is aware of the slightest sound, the smallest thought. The natural conclusion to be drawn is that Awareness is always in a state of perfect peace for complete stillness and total silence is perfect peace.

16/ Notice that Awareness is omniscient, in that every thought/mental image/sensation appears in it, exists in it, is known by it, and disappears back into it. Before any particular thought or sensation there is effortless Awareness of 'what is' (the sum of all thoughts and sensations occurring at any given instant), during the thought or sensation in question there is effortless Awareness of it within 'what is', and then when it has gone there is still effortless Awareness of 'what is'.

17/ Finally notice that every thought/mental image/sensation is 'seen' by the 'light' of Awareness, i.e. Awareness is radiant.[48]

So now we have reached the 'Radiant, still, silent, omnipresent, omniscient, ocean of effortless, choiceless, Awareness' (The Absolute without form or attributes) which, at the deepest level, we all are! Thus the mind, an expression of the beloved, has come to 'know' (more about) Awareness, the lover.

Therefore, the body/mind - itself an ephemeral manifestation of consciousness in motion, the beloved – is an instrument, or conduit, through which the lover can 'know' and love the beloved, and through which the beloved can 'know' and love the lover. Thus The Absolute, consciousness, the union of lover and beloved, can love itself in both 'modes' – at rest or in motion – each 'mode' loving the other.

Feeling you my love.

---

[48] C. Drake, *Beyond the Separate Self,* 2009, Tomewin, p.20-22

Love Loving Itself

Hearing you my love.

Smelling you my love.

Tasting you my love.

Seeing you my love.

Imagining you my love.

Thinking of you my love.

Knowing you my love.

Loving you my love.

In which the 'doer' is pure Awareness, the lover, and that which is being addressed is the manifestation, the beloved. The instrument, body/mind, itself an ephemeral manifestation of the beloved, is the conduit through which love is loving itself.

Feeling you my love.

Hearing you my love.

Smelling you my love.

Tasting you my love.

Seeing you my love.

Imagining you my love.

Thinking of you my love.

Knowing you my love.

Loving you my love.

As you arise from this exercise let it continue, effortlessly, as long as it may, treating every thought and sensation with, and as, love. This will ultimately culminate in being totally in love with existence itself, in which there is nothing but love …

Just to show that this is not an exercise which requires that one be a spiritual adept there is a story about one of the first soviet cosmonauts which illustrates this. It seems that some external equipment on the Soyuz spacecraft became loose and was continually knocking on the windscreen. This was driving him mad and he thought that he would not be able to handle it for the long period he would be orbiting the earth. However, he then had the realization that all he had to do was to learn to love this sound … which he did and this solved the problem![49]

In this there can be no separate 'saying',
The universe is the Lover and Beloved playing.
What may appear to us as 'you' and 'me',
Are expressions, and instruments, of the Totality.

Between Awareness and the Manifestation,
There can be no separation,
For the Lover and Beloved are always one,
Appearing as the many just for fun

---

[49] C.Drake, *Awakening and Beyond*, 2011, Tomewin, p. 166-177

Twenty Five – Loving The Beloved

In this chapter the previous practice is expanded into one in which the senses are enjoyed, or loved by the lover, one at a time and then 'laid over' the preceding one(s), so that at the end the lover is enjoying all five senses together.

In the previous chapter 'Love Loving Itself' I described a method for experiencing the Absolute (Pure Awareness – Consciousness at rest – the deepest level of our being - the lover) loving the beloved (the manifestation – Consciousness in motion) using the physical body as its instrument for this. In this process one focuses on each sense at a time:

> If you like light some subtle incense to add to the atmosphere in the room and brush your teeth (or eat something pleasant) to ensure that there is an agreeable taste in the mouth. Then lie, or sit, in the <u>most comfortable position you can possibly find</u>, with your eyes closed. Make sure that the phone is off the hook and that the 'do not disturb' sign is on the door.

> 1/ Notice the sensations (and feelings) in, and on the surface of, the body. Sink into these sensations, really luxuriate in them as much as possible. Ignore all other sense impressions and thoughts except these sensations.

> (If it appeals you may mentally repeat *Feeling you my love* as you do this.)

> Realize that these occur, are detected by the nervous system, processed by the brain and are then 'seen' by awareness – i.e. you become 'aware' of them.

So the body/mind (itself a manifestation of cosmic energy – the beloved) is an instrument through which awareness-consciousness at rest, the lover – can feel the external world – consciousness in motion, the beloved.

If this is continued with for some time, before moving on to the next sense, one starts to feel the bliss of embodiment – the rhythmic beating of the heart, the blood pumping through the veins, the air on one's face, the warmth in one's feet, sensations of the touching points where the body is in contact with the ground (cushion, pillow, mattress etc.) and so on. The more one can sink into, and luxuriate in, these sensations the stronger the practice becomes.

Once one has 'mastered' this one sense at a time approach, in which one feels that one is 'loving the beloved', then one can begin to overlay the senses on top of each other. So firstly one feels the beloved as deeply as possible and then, whilst maintaining this, one adds hearing the beloved. This is a bit tricky at first, but if one is feeling the bliss previously described then just continue this whilst noticing the sounds in and around the body ... Then this is hearing, whilst also feeling, the beloved.

As you do this realize that each sound is just another vibration, movement, in Consciousness ... and so is the beloved 'vocalizing' ... humming, crooning, singing, yodeling etc. With this realization one can learn to receive each sound with deep affection as an expression of the beloved. If it appeals you may mentally repeat *Feeling you my love , Hearing you my love* as you do this. This entails 'loving the beloved' in another way in addition to loving feeling the beloved. In fact one starts to feel that one is 'making love' to multiple beloveds!

This can then be maintained as one brings (some of) one's attention to the aromas in the room, once again recognizing that these are another way that the beloved manifests ... You can regard these as the perfume (or aftershave!) that the beloved has applied to enhance her (his) appeal. If it appeals you may mentally repeat *Feeling you my love , Hearing you my love , Smelling you my love* as you do this. As you start to enjoy these aromas really bask in them whilst maintaining the sensual bliss and the joy of hearing the beloved.

Next, whilst continuing the above, notice the taste in the mouth and see this as one of the flavors of the beloved. If it appeals you may mentally repeat *Feeling you my love , Hearing you my love , Smelling you my love, Tasting you my love* as you do this. Whilst savoring this realize that this is yet another way that the lover – Pure Awareness – can utilize the body as an instrument to experience the manifest world – the beloved. So now there is simultaneous awareness of feeling, hearing, smelling and tasting the beloved(s).

Finally open your eyes, whilst maintaining some attention on the previous senses and the bliss that their 'detections' entail, and see the beloved. As you do this recognize that every form is a manifestation of cosmic energy – Consciousness in motion – and thus the beloved! This allows one to see everything with a deep affection, or love, seeing their uniqueness and beauty whilst also knowing that they are of the one essence.

If it appeals you may mentally repeat *Feeling you my love , Hearing you my love , Smelling you my love, Tasting you my love, Seeing you my love* as you do this. So the body/mind (itself a manifestation of cosmic energy – the beloved) is an instrument through which awareness- consciousness at rest, the lover – can sense the external world – consciousness in motion, the beloved. Spend some time in reverie and contemplation of this 'seeing' and 'knowing' whilst also being aware of the input from the other sense organs.

This is the final way of using the physical body to 'make love to the beloved' and the focusing on the input from the combination of all five senses is akin to making love to five beloveds simultaneously! Or making love to the one beloved with the whole of your being …

Feeling you my love.
Hearing you my love.
Smelling you my love.

Tasting you my love.

Seeing you my love.

Loving you my love.

A truly blissful experience … and one I can whole heartedly recommend!! As you arise from this exercise let it continue, effortlessly, as long as it may, treating every sensation with, and as, love. This will ultimately culminate in being totally in love with existence itself, in which there is nothing but love …[50]

---

[50] C.Drake, *The Happiness That Needs Nothing*, 2014, Tomewin, p. 113-117

Twenty Six – On Satsang and Other Info

In which I answer the question 'do you give Satsang?' and enclose other information regarding accessing more articles, poems, book info and reviews, my interview on youtube and joining my email group.

Here is an email exchange in which I answer, in the negative, the oft asked question 'do you give Satsang?'

Dear Colin,

Since some month, I am receiving your free emails, which I enjoy tremendously and I m very grateful for!

You directing and reminding me to the truth I Am......

My question is do you give Satsang? If yes, where and when? Are you living here in Australia?

I really would feel blessed, if I could attend your meetings!

Infinite Love and Gratitude. XXXX

Dear XXXX, I am very happy to hear that you enjoy my emails and find them helpful and if I held meetings you would be very welcome to attend. I do not for a few reasons:

1: What I am writing about is so simple that it only requires the reader to follow 'the prompts' whilst investigating for themselves and then to 'honour' what is revealed. The title of my latest 'Honouring The Obvious[51]' encapsulates this ... attached if you missed it.

2: I live between Byron Bay, which is already well served with Satsang givers - Isaac Shapiro (from the Papaji stable) comes to mind but there

---

[51] Chapter eighteen in this book.

are many more.... (In fact Gangaji, my prompter in 1996, is in town as I write!) and the Gold Coast which is not interested ... in Satsang that is. On this subject here is something I wrote (in 'Simply Free to Be') back in 2000:

I finally decided to hold my own meeting to proclaim this truth that I am writing. I directly informed over 700 people by mail or e-mail, advertised in three newspapers and had the meeting announced at the local Theosophical Society, which was to be the venue. Only one person showed up, whom I knew so we just went to her house for a cup of tea, and my reaction was to find it really funny!

3: I live in a stunning location and am naturally very laid back (lazy) so tend to 'do nothing' when I get the chance ... for more on this see attached (The Apparent Elasticity of Time) from *'Awareness of Awareness - The Open Way'*.

So now you know! However, I am always happy to answer questions ... as you can see ... for this is a threefold boon, for me (I love writing and questions often open up new paths for investigation), for chapters in my next book and hopefully for the questioner ... Also, if you are ever in this 'neck of the woods' I am happy for you to come and see me, Love, Colin

If you are interested in more articles, poems, or all formats (paperback, .pdf and epub) of books, including in the new book, *The Simplicity of Awakening – Pointers to The Ease of Being,* these may be found at http://www.lulu.com/spotlight/ColinDrake. If you wish to purchase a book always check www.lulu.com for discounts/sale prices which Lulu is constantly offering.

For example:

Don't Miss Out On Free Shipping!

> Get free mail shipping or 50% off ground shipping on your order.

> Cannot be combined with other offers.

> Offer ends **June 4th at 11:59pm**

> Use Code: JUNESHIP at 'Coupon Code'.

Note that these offers are continually changing and thus needed to be checked before each purchase.

Also all of my books are now available in Kindle format from www.amazon.com and as Ibooks from the Apple store. For more information and an enlarged profile visit www.amazon.com/author/colin_drake

And my youtube interview with Conscious TV is viewable at

https://www.youtube.com/watch?v=Ey_ECAtfdS4

If you have any comments, questions, feedback or to join my email group and receive (free) all new articles and poems as they are posted just email me at colinj108@gmail.com .

Twenty Seven – A Morning Contemplation/Relaxation

Just to get the book back on track, an example of a morning's contemplation/relaxation into 'awareness of Awareness'.

This morning when I lay down in my camper van for my early morning contemplation/relaxation into 'awareness of Awareness' my mind was going a million miles per hour and I thought (incorrectly, see 'Restless mind no problem!' in *A Light Unto Your Self)* this does not augur well … For a bit I just let it do it's own thing (luckily I do know that I am not my mind, hereafter denoted by 'it', so I do not buy into its fantasies) quite amused by its speed at jumping from one topic to another (seemingly unrelated) theme and the utter irrelevance of its creations!

After a while I just inserted the thought (and realisation) that 'there's nothing to achieve for Awareness is already here' which was obvious for I had been (and was) effortlessly aware of its machinations. The effect was electric for this immediately removed any angst regarding the utility of my practice for there was nothing I was trying to achieve … I then allowed it to career on hurtling, this way and that, but with a deeper feeling of relaxation and amusement.

Next I inserted the oxymoron (sometimes needed for it can be pretty moronic!) that 'there is nothing to find for Awareness is already here … and therefore not lost'[52]. Once again it 'stopped' to consider this before resuming its charge but 'enlightened' by the knowledge that it was not searching for anything just having a good time!

---

[52] In fact That's always here and can never be lost, just overlooked to our great cost.

208

Finally, I added the undeniable (it's pretty dumb at times and can only see the obvious) 'there's nothing to desire, get or acquire as That (which you would desire, get or acquire) – Awareness- is already here'. This also brought it shuddering to a halt as the full significance (of nothing to achieve, find or get) fully sank in. And before it could resume its meanderings I threw in:

Pure Awareness,

Consciousness at rest,

In This Aware Nothingness,

All appears to manifest.

Which seemed quite pertinent for it became clear that all of its manifestations (fantasies) were appearing in this Awareness which was at rest and not a 'thing' but the constant, conscious, subjective presence.

Next, whilst this was sinking in, I socked it with:

Radiant Awareness,

Consciousness at rest,

By This Dazzling Darkness,

All is seen which manifests.

Which also seemed self-apparent as its manifestations were seen by the 'light' of Awareness which was a radiance rather than a physical light; for by definition, Consciousness at rest is always in (dazzling) darkness as 'light' is vibration and thus in motion.

Finally as the validity, and consequences, of this were being considered I finished it off with:

> Serene Pristine Awareness,
>
> From which all things are 'lent',
>
> Into This Aware Nothingness
>
> All return when totally 'spent'.

For Awareness is always serene, being at rest, and pristine, being unaffected by whatever comes and goes within It. All things are 'lent' from This as they arise in This, abide in This, are spied by This and subside (when 'spent' – out of energy/motion) back into This.

I then stopped interfering and allowed it (the mind) to carry on regardless whilst noting that everything appearing in it just comes and goes in Awareness which is ever-present, aware of its machinations and every sensation in the body. It soon became completely clear that this stream of ever moving objects flows effortlessly through Awareness, whilst having its source and termination in That and is seen by the radiance of That. Not only that, but as this is the way that we experience the physical world, then this applies to everything in existence! This is backed up by the fact that everything is composed of energy which is always in motion arising from, existing in a substratum of, and returning (when spent) to stillness. So this is true not only of our direct experience but in the physical fact of the way that the universe exists.

As this was going on I felt that I was floating in (and as) a radiant ocean of Consciousness in which all of its creations were appearing, being illuminated and 'seen', and subsiding. As the ocean I was not it (the mind) but also I was not apart from it for it was appearing in me. The difference being that I was (and am!) the never changing Awareness (Consciousness at rest) in which all things, cosmic energy (Consciousness in motion), were coming and going, ebbing and flowing, leaving This totally unaffected.

So much for the restless mind auguring a poor contemplation when it actually pointed directly at the pure Awareness it was appearing in ... as does everything in manifestation if considered in this way!

Appendix One - Investigation of Experience

This gives the basic format for investigating one's moment to moment experience which leads to the conclusion that, at the deepest level, one **is** Awareness.

Below follows a simple method to investigate the nature of reality starting with one's day-to-day experience. Each step should be considered until one experiences, or 'sees', its validity before moving on to the following step. If you reach a step where you do not find this possible, continue on regardless in the same way, and hopefully the flow of the investigation will make this step clear. By all means examine each step critically but with an open mind, for if you only look for 'holes' that's all you will find!

1. Consider the following statement: 'Life, for each of us, is just a series of moment-to-moment experiences'. These experiences start when we are born and continue until we die, rushing headlong after each other, so that they seem to merge into a whole that we call 'my life'. However, if we stop to look we can readily see that, for each of us, every moment is just an experience.

2. Any moment of experience has only three elements: thoughts (including all mental images), sensations (everything sensed by the body and its sense organs) and Awareness of these thoughts and sensations. Emotions and feelings are a combination of thought and sensation.

3. Thoughts and sensations are ephemeral, that is they come and go, and are objects, i.e. 'things' that are perceived.

4. Awareness is the constant subject, the 'perceiver' of thoughts and sensations and that which is always present. Even during sleep there is Awareness of dreams and of the quality of that sleep; and there is also Awareness of sensations; if a sensation becomes strong enough, such as a sound or uncomfortable sensation, one will wake up.

5. All thoughts and sensations appear in Awareness, exist in Awareness, and subside back into Awareness. Before any particular thought or sensation there is effortless Awareness of 'what is': the sum of all thoughts and sensations occurring at any given instant. During the thought or sensation in question there is effortless Awareness of it within 'what is'. Then when it has gone there is still effortless Awareness of 'what is'.

6. So the body/mind is experienced as a flow of ephemeral objects appearing in this Awareness, the ever present subject. For each of us any external object or thing is experienced as a combination of thought and sensation, i.e. you may see it, touch it, know what it is called, and so on. The point is that for us to be aware of anything, real or imaginary, requires thought about and/or sensation of that thing and it is Awareness of these thoughts and sensations that constitutes our experience.

7. Therefore this Awareness is the constant substratum in which all things appear to arise, exist and subside. In addition, all living things

rely on Awareness of their environment to exist and their behaviour is directly affected by this. At the level of living cells and above this is self-evident, but it has been shown that even electrons change their behaviour when (aware of) being observed! Thus this Awareness exists at a deeper level than body/mind (and matter/energy[53]) and *we are this Awareness*!

8. This does not mean that at a surface level we are not the mind and body, for they arise in, are perceived by and subside back into Awareness, which is the deepest and most fundamental level of our being. However, if we choose to identify with this deepest level – Awareness - (the perceiver) rather than the surface level, mind/body (the perceived), then thoughts and sensations are seen for what they truly are, just ephemeral objects which come and go, leaving Awareness itself totally unaffected.

9. Next investigate this Awareness itself to see whether its properties can be determined.
Firstly what is apparent is that this Awareness is effortlessly present and effortlessly aware. It requires no effort by the mind/body and thoughts and sensations cannot make it vanish however hard they try.

10. Next, this Awareness is choicelessly present and choicelessly aware. Once again it requires no choice of the mind/body and they

---

[53] The theory of relativity, and string theory, show that matter and energy are synonymous.

cannot block it however they try. For example, if you have a toothache there is effortless Awareness of it and the mind/body cannot choose for this not to be the case. You may think that this is bad news but it is not so: can you imagine if you had to make a choice whether you would like to be aware of every sensation that the body experiences? In fact be grateful that there is no effort or choice involved for Awareness just to be - such ease and simplicity - which is not surprising for you are this Awareness!

11. It can be seen then, that for each of us this Awareness is omnipresent; we never experience a time or place when it is not present. Once again be grateful that the mind/body is never required to search for this Awareness; it is just always there, which of course is not surprising for at the deepest level we are this Awareness.

12. Next, notice that this Awareness is absolutely still for it is aware of the slightest movement of body or mind. For example, we all know that to be completely aware of what is going on around us in a busy environment we have to be completely still, just witnessing the activity.

13. In the same vein this Awareness is totally silent as it is aware of the slightest sound and the smallest thought.

14. In fact this Awareness is totally without attributes for all attributes occur in and are noticed by their lack, i.e. sounds occur in silence, exist in silence, are noticed by their contrast to silence, and disappear back

into silence; forms occur in space, exist in space, are noticed by their contrast to space, disappear back into space, and so on.

15. It can be easily seen that this Awareness is totally pure; it is unaffected by whatever occurs in it, in the same way that a cinema screen is unaffected by any movie shown on it, however gross or violent. In fact no 'thing' can taint Awareness; for by definition Awareness cannot be affected by any 'thing', as all 'things' are just ephemeral objects which appear in, exist in and finally disappear back into Awareness, the constant subject.

16. This Awareness is omniscient; everything appears to arise in it, to exist in it, is known by it and to subside back into it.

17. Finally, it seems that this Awareness is forever radiant; it illuminates whatever occurs in it, thus the mind can see it, i.e. become conscious of it.

18. When one identifies with this Awareness, there is nothing (in terms of enlightenment or Awakening) to achieve, or struggle towards, for how can one achieve what one already is?
All that is required is for the mind to recognize that one is this Awareness.

19. When one identifies with this Awareness there is nothing to find, for how can one find what cannot be lost? All that is required is for the mind to stop overlooking what is always present, that which perceives the mind and body.

20. When one identifies with this Awareness, there is nothing to desire, long for or get, for how can one get what already is? All that is required is for the mind to realize that which one already is: Pure Awareness.

So now we have reached the 'Pure, radiant, still, silent, omnipresent, omniscient, ocean of effortless, choiceless, attributeless Awareness' which we all are! Give up all striving, seeking and desiring, and just identify with This which you already are. Identification with This, rather than with body/mind (thought/sensations), gives instant peace, for Awareness is always still and silent, totally unaffected by whatever appears in it.

Although we, in essence, are 'The pure, radiant, still, silent, omnipresent, omniscient, ocean of effortless, choiceless, attributeless Awareness' it is impossible to experience this: we can know it or realize it but it is beyond the realm of experience. This is because all experience appears in This, exists in This and dissolves back into This. In much the same way that you do not see the cinema screen whilst the movie is playing, this pure screen of Awareness cannot be seen by the mind, i.e. experienced, whilst the movie of mind/body is playing on it.

218

The only way it is possible to see the screen is when no movie is playing, but as *experience is the movie* this pure screen of Awareness is always outside of the realm of experience.

However, recognition of oneself as this 'pure, radiant, still, silent, omnipresent, omniscient, ocean of effortless, choiceless, attributeless, Awareness' may evoke many experiences such as bliss, joy, relaxation (what a relief that there's no individual 'me me me'), a lifting of a great burden, i.e. enlightenment in the literal sense of the word, universal love etc. These experiences vary greatly from person to person and are ultimately irrelevant as the recognition and realization of one's own essential nature is the crucial factor for attaining freedom.

Note that although we cannot experience our essence, we can absolutely know it* just as we know, without a doubt, that the screen is there (when we watch a movie). Then however terrifying, gripping or moving the movie is we are not shaken because we know it is a movie. We still enjoy it, in fact we enjoy it even more, because it is just pure entertainment and we are not totally identified with it. In the same way, once we know our essential nature, life can be seen as a movie and enjoyed as such without identifying ourselves as being trapped in it. Thus, although we cannot experience our essence, once we recognize it all of our experiences are transformed by no longer identifying with them but just enjoying them, or accepting them as ephemeral states which come and go. When viewed like this, thoughts and sensations lose their power to overwhelm us, as we stop buying into them as indicators of who or what we are. They are just like waves on the ocean or clouds in the sky, which appear and disappear leaving the ocean or the sky unaffected.

*Just as you could not see a movie without the screen, you could not experience anything without Awareness, for without that what would there be to experience? For without that we would see nothing (there would be no Awareness of what was seen), hear nothing, feel nothing, taste nothing, smell nothing and not know our own thoughts! In fact, experience on any level would not be possible.[54]

Awareness can also be defined as universal consciousness when it is totally at rest, completely still; aware of every movement that is occurring within it. In our direct experience we can see that Awareness is still, as there is Awareness of the slightest movement of mind or body. In fact this is the 'stillness' relative to which any movement can be known. Every 'thing' that is occurring in consciousness is a manifestation of cosmic energy, for the string theory[55] and the earlier theory of relativity show that matter is in fact energy, which is consciousness in motion (or motion in consciousness). For energy is synonymous with motion and consciousness is the substratum, or deepest level, of all existence.

---

[54] C. Drake, *Beyond The Separate Self,* 2009, Tomewin, p.18-25
[55] This posits that all 'things' are composed of 'strings' of energy in complex configurations, vibrating at various frequencies.

Now all motion arises in stillness, exists in stillness, is known by its comparison with stillness, and eventually subsides back into stillness. For example, if you walk across a room, before you start there is stillness, as you walk the room is still and you know you are moving relative to this stillness, and when you stop once again there is stillness. In the same way every 'thing' (consciousness in motion) arises in Awareness (consciousness at rest), exists in Awareness, is known in Awareness and subsides back into Awareness. Awareness is still, but is the container of all potential energy which is continually bubbling up into manifestation (physical energy) and then subsiding back into stillness. [56]

---

[56] C. Drake, *Light Unto Your Self,* 2011, Tomewin, p.75-76

Appendix Two - Instruments of The Absolute

An investigation which reveals that our mind/bodies are instruments of The Absolute, that is the Pure Awareness, through which It can experience, know, and enjoy Its physical manifestation – the universe.

If you sit quietly noticing the sensations in (and on the surface of) your body, you can easily see that these occur, are detected by the nervous system and then appear in Awareness, i.e. you become aware of them.

In the same vein you can notice that sounds occur, are detected by the ears, and then appear in Awareness.

Sights occur, are detected by the eyes, and then appear in Awareness.

Aromas occur, are detected by the nose, and then appear in Awareness.

Flavours occur, are detected by the taste buds and then appear in Awareness.

Thoughts occur, are detected by the mind, and then appear in Awareness.

Mental images occur, are detected by the mind, and then appear in Awareness.

Therefore the physical mind/body is an instrument through which Awareness (consciousness at rest) can sense and contemplate the physical manifestation of cosmic energy (consciousness in motion, or motion in consciousness).

So the body/mind is an instrument through which Awareness can experience the physical world, for experience *is* Awareness of thoughts/mental images/sensations.

The body/mind is also an instrument through which Awareness can interact with, and enjoy, the universal manifestation of cosmic energy.

Thus the body/mind is an instrument through which consciousness can 'know itself' when manifest as the physical world, that is when in motion.

The human mind has the added advantage of being capable of 'self realization' that is of realizing the deeper level of 'Pure Awareness', consciousness at rest, the unmanifest.

Therefore the human mind/body is an instrument through which consciousness can 'know itself' in both 'modes': at rest and in motion. That is as 'Pure Awareness' and as the physical universe.

This realization of humans as instruments of the divine (consciousness) occurs in many of the world's religions. In Judaism, as instruments to enjoy and continue the creation; in Islam, as instruments through which Allah could know Himself; in Advaita Vedanta, as instruments through which Brahman could know Himself and His manifestation; and in Vaishnavism, as instruments to perform Yagnas (sacrifices) for the satisfaction of Krishna (Vishnu). There are also echoes of this in Christianity where man can be seen as an instrument to glorify God and receive His benefits. Mahayana Buddhism also has the concept of the Bodhisattva as an instrument to work for the enlightenment of all beings.

This is particularly stressed in Advaita Vedanta where we find the idea delineated in the Upanishads:

> As Brahman is everything, it follows that we all are Brahman and that He is the agent by which the mind thinks, eye sees, tongue speaks, ear hears and body breathes (*Kena* I v.5-9). He is also described as the 'ear of the ear, eye of the eye, mind of the mind, word of the words and life of the life' (*Kena* I v.2). Thus He is the 'Pure Awareness' (*Brihadaranyaka* 4 v.7) in which all thought, life and sensation appears; and He is the 'seer' (*Isha* v.8) and 'all knowing' (*Katha* 2 v.18).
> The Katha Upanishad likens man to a chariot, of which the atman (the Self, Awareness, Brahman within each individual) is the master, the body is the chariot, the mind is the charioteer, the sense organs are the horses and the roads they travel on are the objects of sensation. The atman is the enjoyer and experiencer of the ride, which is made possible by the charioteer, chariot and horses. (Katha Upanishad 3v.3-4) So Brahman needs the mind and senses, to enjoy and experience the physical world.

However, when the mind is unaware of the master's presence, through lack of discrimination, it is unable to control the senses which run amok like wild horses (Ibid 3v.5). Brahman, pure consciousness, is hidden in every heart, being the eternal witness watching everything one does. He is said to be 'the operator' whilst we are his 'innumerable instruments'. (Svetasvetara Upanishad 6v.10-12)

Moreover, it is not only humans but all 'sensing' organisms that are instruments through which consciousness can 'know itself' when manifest as the physical world, that is when in motion.

Obviously different organisms have different capacities in this respect as all senses are limited to certain wavelengths, or range, of sensation (experience). As far as we know humans are the only species capable of 'self realization' that is of realizing the deeper level of 'Pure Awareness', consciousness at rest, and thus are the only beings through which consciousness can 'know itself' when at rest as Pure Awareness. However, there could well be other species, terrestrial and non-terrestrial, that are capable of this. Humans are also only limited instruments in terms of sensing, contemplating and 'knowing' the manifest and the unmanifest.

The Author – A short spiritual biography

I was born into a strict, but joyful, Methodist family. From the ages of 11-17 I was sent to a Methodist boarding school, which I left with the conviction that organized Christianity was not for me. I could see that what Christ said about living was wonderful, but that the church did not really promote his teachings rather concentrating on him as our 'saviour' and on the purportedly 'miraculous' facets of his life. It was also very apparent that many so called Christians were not interested in practicing what he taught.

This was now 1965 and living in central London during the years of flower-power I experimented with various hallucinogens, finding them very beneficial for opening my subconscious which allowed years of conditioning to pour out. This left me: feeling totally 'cleansed' and unburdened, ready to start life anew in a spirit of investigation as to the nature of reality. The psychedelic states also presaged, gave a glimpse of, mystical states which I suspected were attainable through spiritual practices.

I then embarked on a study of Gurdjieff and Ouspensky which I found absolutely fascinating and was convinced that self-realization was the purpose of life. However, they made the process sound so onerous that (being young, foot-loose and fancy-free) I decided to shelve the whole project temporarily.

It was not until eight years later that I resumed the spiritual search when Janet (my partner) introduced me: to my first yoga-teacher, Matthew O'Malveny, who inspired us by quoting passages from the Upanishads, Dhammapada, and other scriptures during the class. He also emphasized the importance of relaxation and meditation. There followed a few years of investigating various spiritual paths including a prolonged dalliance with the Brahma Kumaris (Raja Yoga) whose meditations were wonderful, but whose dogma was very hard to take.

We then moved into the country to start a pottery and immersed ourselves in Satyananda Yoga, an organization which had no dogma but taught a wide range of yogic practices. We were both initiated into *karma sannyas* by Swami Satyananda and adopted a yogic lifestyle consisting of asanas, pranayama, yoga nidra, meditation, kirtan and vegetarianism.

During this time I was at a silent retreat when I happened to pick up a volume entitled *The Gospel of Ramakrishna* which introduced me: to this amazing being who practiced many spiritual paths, within Hinduism and also Islam and Christianity, discovering that they all lead to the same result. He was then approached by many devotees from these various paths all of whom he was able to teach in their own path, whilst emphasizing the harmony of religions. A few years later I was lucky enough to find an erudite nun in the Sarada Ramakrishna Order, based in Sydney, who initiated me: into the worship of this amazing being. This entailed two to three hours of daily meditation, *japa* (mantra repetition)

228

during daily activities, reading every word said by or written about him, including daily readings of *The Gospel of Sri Ramakrishna*, and chanting. I continued this sadhana quite happily for ten years.

I then encountered a disciple of Sri Ramana Maharshi, Gangaji, who said 'Stop! Be still, you are already That'. The message being that the effort and search were masking that which is always present; all that was required was to 'stop' and see what is always here. After many years of struggle and effort this news came like a breath of fresh air and I glimpsed the essence, that undeniable ever-present reality. This was followed by a seven day silent retreat which resulted in my first 'Awakening', and also in an ecstasy that slowly faded over the following year.

My first book *Beyond the Separate Self, The End of Anxiety and Mental Suffering* came about from the realization that occurred then and has matured over the following 12 years. During this time I wrote a series of articles, for an e-mail news group, based on my meditations and contemplations, around which that book is based. At the same time I have also completed an honours degree in comparative religion and philosophy, using the insights gained by my spiritual practices to inform my essays. Some of these essays were adapted to include as chapters in that book.

My honours thesis, together with an essay about Ramakrishna used to highlight the themes explored, has now also been published by www.nonduality.com under the title: *Humanity, Our Place in the*

Universe, The Central Beliefs of the World's Religions. I have also continued writing articles and replying to questions which has resulted in more books. As this is written there are thirteen, including this book:

Beyond The Separate Self - The End of Anxiety and Mental Suffering 2009

A Light Unto Your Self - Self Discovery Through Investigation of Experience 2011

Awakening and Beyond - Self Recognition and its Consequences 2012

Awareness of Awareness - The Open Way 2013

The Happiness That Needs Nothing - Pointers to That Which is Always Here 2014

Freedom From Anxiety and Needless Suffering – Pointers and Practices to Aid Awakening 2015

The first five are also available in poetry form, one poem per chapter, entitled 'Poetry From *Book Title Name*'. Plus the aforementioned book comparing the world's major religions and how they define Humanity's essence and 'place' in the universe:

Humanity - Our Place in the Universe - The Central Belief's of the World's Religions 2010

So, as you can see, I always have at least two books in the pipeline, without necessarily intending to write more 'books', due to the replies, articles and poems that are being written. There is another book of poems almost completed, and I have some articles for the following one already 'squirreled' away ... The books have also been made available in all formats, hard-copy, .pdf, epub, and Kindle (.mobi) from various outlets including Amazon, Nook, Ibookstore and many other book stores around the world. Also all of my articles and poems are distributed freely to my email group (which all are welcome to join at colin108@dodo.com.au) normally before they are incorporated into a book.

One further point that I would like to make is that writing the books has been an absolute blessing for me as it has unfolded over the years. The recording of the discoveries, answering questions, and the honing of the texts, has been a joy and has increased and prolonged my periods of 'wakefulness'. On re-reading the manuscripts so many times, for editing and verification purposes, I have come to realize that I (the separate self) do not write them at all but that they come from, and through, this limited manifestation of Pure Awareness. As such they are bound to contain some errors due to the limitedness of the manifestation, but hopefully these will become corrected as further discoveries occur. Thus they will always be 'works in progress', which is wonderful for it will spur me: on to overcome its limitations by further investigation, contemplation and meditation. So I would absolutely encourage you, the reader, to record your own discoveries, and never be totally content with what you have written, so that your record will inspire you and encourage you to deeper investigation/contemplation/meditation.

If you wish to contact me: with any questions or feedback you may do so at <u>colin108@dodo.com.au</u>

Glossary

Some of the following terms may not have been used in this book, although they have in the preceding ones, and I have included them as you may find them useful in future reading on this subject.

Advaita: non-dual.

Arhat: One who seeks liberation by attaining Nibbana.

Anatta: no individual separate self.

Anicca: impermanence.

Atman: Brahman within each individual, that portion of The Absolute in each person.

Bodhisattva: one who seeks full enlightenment so as to aid others to do the same.

Brahman: the all-pervading transcendental Absolute Reality.

Darshan: the blessing or purification felt in the presence of holiness.

Dukkha: 'Suffering' or the general unsatisfactoriness of existence.

Hinyana: the 'lesser vehicle' a derogatory term coined by followers of Mahayana for teachings designed for Arhats – those who seek personal liberation.

Kali: the Divine Mother, creator, preserver and destroyer. Sakti, cosmic energy, consciousness in motion.

Lila: the divine play or manifestation, consciousness in motion.

Mahayana: the 'great vehicle' capable of carrying many people to liberation, as a bodhisattva is one who vows not to enter into *parinirvana* until all creatures are liberated.

Maya: The power of Brahman, which supports the cosmic illusion of the One appearing as the many.

Nibbana or Nirvana: Buddhist words for *moksa*, enlightenment, Awakening.

Nitya: the Ultimate Reality, the eternal Absolute.

Parinirvana: The nirvana that a fully enlightened being enters after death, from which there is no reincarnation.

Prakriti: the manifestation, nature.

Purusa: the witnessing consciousness, or Awareness, according to Samkhya unique to each individual.

Sakti: cosmic energy, consciousness in motion.

Satchitananda: existence (*sat*), consciousness (*chit*), bliss (*ananda*).

Siva: universal consciousness when it is at rest, aware of every movement occurring in it, which is 'Pure Awareness'.

Theravada: 'Doctrine of the Elders' – Teachings based on Buddha's direct teachings.

Upanishads: the last works of the Vedas, in which ritual was supplanted by the personal and mystical experiencing of The Absolute (Brahman).

Vinaya: The monastic code for Theravadan Buddhist monks.

Bibliography

Barks C., *The Essential Rumi,* 1995, Penguin, Harmondsworth

Conze E., *Buddhist Scriptures* '1959 Penguin Books, Harmondsworth

Drake C., *A Light Unto Your Self,* 2011, Beyond Awakening Publications, Tomewin

Drake C., *Awakening and Beyond,* 2012, Beyond Awakening Publications, Tomewin

Drake C., *Awareness of Awareness,* 2013, Beyond Awakening Publications, Tomewin

Drake C., *Beyond The Separate Self,* 2009, Beyond Awakening Publications, Tomewin

Drake C., *Freedom From Anxiety and Needless Suffering,* 2015, Beyond Awakening Publications, Tomewin

Drake C., *Humanity - Our Place in The Universe,* 2010, Beyond Awakening Publications, Tomewin

Drake C., *Poetry From Beyond The Separate Self,* 2012, Beyond Awakening Publications, Tomewin

Drake C., *The Happiness That Needs Nothing,* 2014, Beyond Awakening Publications, Tomewin

Drake C., *The Simplicity of Awakening,* 2016, Beyond Awakening Publications, Tomewin

Easwaran E., *The Dhammapadda,* 1986, Blue Mountain Center of Meditation, Berkley

Gombrich R.F., *Theravada Buddhism,* 1988, Routledge & Kegan Paul, London

Harvey P., *An introduction to Buddhism,* 1990, Cambridge Uni Press, Cambridge

Friedlander P., *Buddhism Past and Present* , 2002, La Trobe Uni, Melbourne Vic.

Goldstein J., *The Experience of Insight* , 1987 Shambala, Boston Mass.

RELS301 Unit Notes, *Religious Literature,* 2004, U.N.E. Armidale NSW

Sw. Prabhavananda, *The Upanishads* , 1968, Sri Ramakrishna Math, Myalpore Madras

Sw. Nikhilanda, *The Gospel of Ramakrishna,* 1942, Ramakrishna Math, Mylapore

Watts A.W., *The Way of Zen*, 1957, Penguin Books, London

Williams P., *Mahayana Buddhism*, 1989 Routledge, London and New York

Williams P., *Buddhist Thought,* 2000, Routledge, London and New York